The COVID BIBLE

DEEP INSIDE THE MIND:

Wisdom from Beyond for the NEW AGE

by **LORAINE REES** and

Dr. Mary Ross

Published by Oxshott Press
Copyright © 2020 M. Ross

All rights reserved. No part of this publication may be reproduced, sorted in a retrieval system or transmitted in any form, and taken out of context except for excerpts to be published with various book reviews, or to support individuals or groups in conducting meditation sessions. We are happy to encourage individual or group meditation sessions.

Part of the proceeds from the sale of each book will go to children's charities.

ISBN: 978 1 7360234-5-7

For more information, you can contact:
Loraine Rees School of Psychic Studies on facebook or:
www.OxshottPress

Other books in this series include:

LOVE AND LAUGHTER WITH MEDIUM LORAINE REES, by Dr. Mary Ross

and

TROUBLED SPIRITS WITH MEDIUM LORAINE REES, by Dr. Mary Ross.

TABLE OF CONTENTS

INTRODUCTION 5
THE NEW ERA 9
ISOLATION 11
SOUL CLUSTERS 21
COVID-19 and THE BODY 23
EMBRACE YOUR HUMANITY 36
RIGHT AND WRONG 39
GUIDANCE FROM THE HIGHER REALMS 41
RESTORING EARTH'S BALANCE 54
RELIGION 60
PRAYER 64
DIFFERENT TYPES OF SOULS 75
OTHER SOULS AMONG YOU 77
DIMENSIONS 79
THE REALMS OF HEAVEN 80
FREE WILL 90
DEATH 92
SPIRIT GUIDES 97
A GUIDED MEDITATION TO THE HIGHER REALMS 99
GUIDED MEDITATION THROUGH THE ASTRAL PLANE 105
THE CHANGING FACE OF RELIGION 113
THE NATURE OF GOD 116
LIVING A POSITIVE LIFE 119
SIGNS AND SEERS 123
MANIFEST YOUR FUTURE 127

TAROT	130
THE SEER WITHIN YOU	133
YOUR PERSONAL RELATIONSHIP WITH GOD	134
IN THE WAKE	141
THE CONSCIOUS AND SUBCONSCIOUS MIND	146
THE GIFT OF DÉJÀ VU	149
ABORTION	153
SAME GENDER RELATIONS	157
ARTIFICIAL INTELLIGENCE	159
SPEAKING IN TONGUES	160
WHY YOU WERE CREATED	161
THE UNIVERSE	166
GOING FORWARD	172
THE SHIFT FROM RELIGION TO SPIRITUALITY	175
ABOUT THE AUTHORS	181

INTRODUCTION

I have been privileged to have been invited into the world and inner workings of the talented medium clairvoyant Loraine Rees, to observe and record the astonishing things that result when she connects to the other side. After writing the first two books about her and her work, in April 2020, during the heart of the pandemic, Loraine was advised by her spirit guides to contact me to discuss a new book. This one wouldn't be about her or her practice but would contain messages directly dictated to her by Spirit.

Loraine has been in contact with the spirit world ever since she was a child. Even coming from a family of clairvoyants, her gift to connect with the other side has been particularly strong. Her first memory as a child was the surprise to learn that her parents could not see "the gray people." She has spent her life passing on the messages she has received. Most of her work involves delivering messages to specific people from loved ones on the other side.

But with a world ravaged by pandemic, the spirit world told her there were bigger messages to deliver. She was told we were to do another book, its contents dictated to her from the other side. This book is the result. This is a series of passages dictated to her directly from the spirit world, from April 2020 through June, 2020. These are messages the spirit world wants us to know – written down and accessible to those of us on this side of life. With the radical changes we have faced in 2020, there has never been a greater need for wisdom from beyond.

As Loraine's biographer, my job is to transcribe what Spirit has dictated to (and through) Loraine, and present it as clearly and accurately as I can. I have known and worked with Loraine for nearly 15 years. She tells me this is a fortuitous and powerful number. I have learned to trust Loraine's ability to connect with the spirit world, as well as her absolute dedication in relaying that information as accurately as she receives it. Sometimes it gets her into trouble if people don't want to hear the message sent from the other side because the truth can be difficult. Still, Loraine never shies away from delivering whatever message she receives. I have come to have the deepest respect for the integrity of her spirit guides that provide the information from the other side, particularly Ramos, her main spirit guide. After watching Loraine work under Ramos' guidance for these past years, I have come to have full trust in the process.

However, I admit I was not prepared for the severity of some of the messages that have come through in these sessions. This book contains the messages Loraine has been given from the spirit world, channeled through her spirit guide Ramos, to be shared with the people on this side of life.

These messages have been delivered to her while in a meditative state, and have often come directly through her throat chakra. As I listen to her tapes and transcribe them, her voice can change dramatically. As Ramos has related to her, some of these messages are quite blunt. This may alienate some people, although that is not the intent. The intent is to help people learn to grow and develop into more spiritual beings while they are here on the earthly plane.

This is the information the spirit world wants us to pass on. We are creating the format, but the content has been given to us from the other side, mainly from channeling Ramos, who in turn has been supported by other spirits on the other side. We serve as conveyors of the information the spirit world wishes us to deliver. We hope that this information assists people in making sense of the new world order. We hope that it helps people form deep connections with their inner minds, to aid them in forming their own powerful bonds with the spirit world and the Universal God. We also hope that it helps people form positive connections with the physical world around them in a way that appreciates and respects their position within it, and helps them live and work in harmony within in.

We particularly hope, that by relating these words from the other side, that we have correctly fulfilled what Spirit has asked us to do. It is our deepest wish that this will help humanity forestall even worse problems for itself. We hope these passages will allow people to understand why this is happening now, and help us all to navigate our way through the new world order, both during this pandemic and in its wake, which will be considerable.

The following chapters have been given to us by Ramos on the other side, and delivered through Loraine. By seeing the world from the other side, it gives us an entirely different way to view it. This is what the spirit world wants us to understand. We hope this new way of seeing things will allow our species to grow and learn what we need to, in order to keep evolving spiritually – and to continue.

- Dr. Mary Ross

THE NEW ERA

This is the start of a new era for you humans, and a time of new beginnings. With that comes the time to consider the bigger picture beyond your physical world view. With so many of you finding yourselves in isolation, in a significant way you are each like Moses in the wilderness, in isolation high up on the mountain top. The current Bible holds only one-fifth of the scriptures that were written. Most of the scriptures were removed or hidden away throughout the ages because those passages didn't suit the purpose of the leaders of organized religion who controlled the written archives. Religion was started to help people learn to worship, but over the years, many of those scriptures have been lost or removed. It is time for the spirit world to dictate new passages and messages to you in the living world. Now is the time for new laws to be written, delivered from the spirit world, that are applicable to the new world order.

It is particularly important to share the knowledge that you can access the spirit world directly and converse with your creator yourself. This does not require an organized religion. You do not need a religious mediator. The means and rules to access the spirit world are simple and free and easy to follow.

You need to realign yourselves in order to re-direct the future of mankind and your planet. It is still possible. You can do this. You must do this. The pandemic is a wake-up call that you should not ignore.

Why are you fighting amongst yourselves? Isn't the pandemic enough of a problem? Your soul has no race or color. All souls are equally important to your creator. All souls are equally loved by your creator. There is still time to save your world. Now is that time.

ISOLATION

In your time scale, as I dictate these words to you, it is spring of 2020. This is a time when many of your people find themselves in some form of self-isolation. People are confused and don't really understand what is going on. Picture sitting on top of a mountain in Biblical days, when prophets received divine message from the other side. Although you are no longer allowed to go up those mountains, in a way, isolation reminds you of those simpler times, feeling apart and alone. Use this time to each create the "mountain of isolation" in your own space. You need to spend time meditating, and find the real purpose of your lives. You need to understand why this little rock you call Earth that floats along with billions of people on it has been abused so badly.

Think back to ancient times. As you walk along, feel yourself climbing up a steep slope. Feel yourself hearing the sounds of animals running and birds flying. You don't spend enough time hearing these sounds because you're so busy on your trains and airplanes, rushing to work. This is the time, children, for you to understand there are higher realms. These realms are beyond your imagination. But know this:

there is one God, who has created you and your world, and has created many other worlds. Your God has a thousand names, but the names do not matter. Just as the word "water" does not get you wet, so the word "God" does not relate to any specific religion. In these pages, "God" will be referred to as the Universal God. This is the universal energy that sustains life. If it wasn't for this God of the Universe, who has created and supported your world for so long, your world would have been destroyed many years ago.

Isolation is not something that you are used to. You're used to turning on the TV and picking up the phones. Even in the time of pandemic, you're not really in isolation. Isolation is when you are completely on your own. Isolation is a meditative state where you become one with your God.

For you people on Earth, you may find it difficult to comprehend that you can connect with the Universal God through isolation. You are born with the ability to socialize with others. You are born in a time with the ability to travel from one side of the world to the other. You are born in a time with the ability to communicate from one side of the world to the other. Think back to the times when the ability to communicate was limited within the village. Beyond each village was a different realm, and no one knew what was going in those other realms. Those other realms were like an alien state, completely unfamiliar to their neighboring states.

You may be thinking this is not making a lot of sense right now. But I must tell you that through the realms of the spirit, you can travel outside your kingdom without technology. You can travel beyond your physical world. You can travel through the spirit realms through your meditation and seek answers. Examples of guided meditations will be given within these pages.

You are not truly alone, because you have the power within you to reach other realms of the spirit world. Although you may be feeling isolated, you are not. By going deep within, you can meditate and be more connected than ever as you become one with your God. By connecting on this deeper level, you will not be alone.

Missing your family is different from being in isolation. Missing your family is a need to feel love and be loved. This is a human need that your God has put inside you to show your humanity to one another. But the humanity of the mankind has been fading. The respect for the plants, the respect for the oceans, the respect for the animals that your Universal God has provided your planet with has become despicable. The respect for your fellow mankind isn't there as it should be. People often walk past people crying in the street. You might pass by someone begging for a scrap of bread or a drink of water. The humanity of this race called humans is in decline. Only 27% of the human population is what could be called humane. The rest say that they are, but they are not. For them, their "God" is not of the spirit world, but of the man-made world. The lust of drugs. The lust of fame. The lust of fortune. They worship their own false idols but pretend to come across very Godly. This may not be what you want to hear right now, but you need to hear it because your world is in pieces. Armageddon is beyond and beyond. Armageddon should have happened before now. The seeds of Armageddon were sewn before the beginning of the 2,000 years since the prophet Jesus Christ walked the earth.

Armageddon is the downfall of religion. Look where religion has gone. Most people claim to belong to a religion, which has become a big part of your lives for so long. Whether you believe in Jesus Christ or Judaism or Buddhism, you have been controlled by organized religion, which have become increasingly rife with false gods and false idols.

Who do you revere? Who do you respect the most? Is it the movie stars, who are interesting to watch? Do you value their views because they are famous? Is it your politicians you respect? Have they chosen those jobs to help others or to benefit their own egos? Is it the financial wizards you respect the most, who have learned to control wealth? Whoever you respect, you must consider why you respect them. Have they done something truly worthy, as human beings, to earn your respect? Or do you wish to emulate them for the type of earthly success they have achieved?

The earthly successes of fame and fortune are temporary. They will fade to nothing and mean nothing when their lives are done and their souls arrive in the spirit world.

When you engage with an organized religion, you enter your own type of isolation. You go to church or the temple and you isolate yourself from the outside world. For those few minutes you believe you are doing something very good for your God. You believe you are doing something powerful for your God. But that is not true. An old building with an abundance of gold and money is not where you find God. Through total isolation and meditation, that is where you will truly find your creator, the Universal God. Enter that meditative state with a pure heart and a pure soul, and the ability to love unconditionally, and that is where you will find your pure God.

In the year 2029 you will experience many disasters on Earth. Most of them will be man-made. Two of them will be natural disasters; this will come to pass. These natural disasters, rooted in water and fire, will arrive from the north and the east. They will result in a global situation. Man-made disasters will follow that will destroy many lives. This will be a very egotistical destruction, once again caused by people in power deciding what is going to happen to the rest of you.

The purpose of isolation, as we know it now, is for souls of like-minded people to connect with the Universe -- and pray deeply to the Universe to help sift out all the good from the bad, and bring pure love back into the world.

Your world is a tiny rock – a very tiny part of the bigger picture of the Universe. But it is a very needy part, and has become spiritually far away from us in the spirit world. We will be watching you, and working out which of your souls will be allowed to carry on and which souls will not.

The soul is something that is inside every living being, every living creature. Every breath you take feeds your soul. Your soul carries on for eternity if it is worthy. If so, it will go up through the realms higher and higher, to embrace other beautiful souls in harmony and engage with incomprehensible joy. But at this moment in time, so many earthly souls are struggling and many of the darker souls want to control you and take your power for themselves.

The ability to heal yourselves is there. The ability in God's garden to heal yourself is there. But your money focuses on treatments and the drugs, and the abilities for your doctors to make a potion to make you better. You have believed in these systems for so long that the current situation comes as a shock. Look at your pharmaceutical companies. Look at the resources they are taking from the planet. Look at how much they are taking in financial resources. If they were truly making these drugs to cure people, they would have done this many years ago.

But their aim is to keep you needy so everyone parts with their money. You have allowed this to happen, and forgotten that everything in God's garden has a cure for you.

Let us return to the concept of isolation. As groups of people gather and meditate, you can bring goodness back into the earth. By combining your meditative sessions with others, you can bring harmony back to your little rock that spins around in this vast Universe. The power of souls, joining together in a meditative state can be so much more powerful than this rock you call Earth, which is really nothing more in the scheme of the Universe than a speck of dust.

During this pandemic isolation, find time to rejoice with the Universe. Take time to find yourself, your true ability, and the love you were born with. Find your passion as you go deep within, and find yourself. Are you worried about your neighbor? The elderly lady with no family? But you can't go knocking on the door to see if she's okay? Or are you more worried that you can't go to the shop and buy a new dress? Are you worried that the street people are not being protected from this virus? Or are you more worried you can't go to work and earn your money?

Spend time in a deep meditation state to discover what really worries you the most. Look at the animal kingdom -- the beauty of these creatures that your Universal God has created. Look at your giraffes. Look at your lions. Look what you've done to their environment. Look at your trophies of rhinoceros and their horns. Are they better off on the shelf or are they better off attached to these living creatures?

Look at your possessions. Look at the dogs you buy as puppies. But once they start becoming a nuisance, do you get rid of them? Do you treat everything in your world as disposable, like garbage? Remember, in your isolation, to take 30 minutes a day to quiet the outside noise. Quiet your mind, and go deep within it and search for your inner self and your God.

I'm also being drawn to the stress of the family, with people living underneath each other's feet in the same houses. Finding little things that annoy you and aggravate you. You think, "Do I really want to be around this person? Do I want to be around my children 24-7?" As a society, your normal lives don't involve sitting at home in groups of people. Your lives have become busy, busy, busy. You don't have time to really know your family. Now is the time to sit down and have real discussions with the ones sheltered with you. The others in your family can be reached by technology. Take the time to phone them up and do simple joyful things. Play games over the internet. Share little moments with them that will make them happy.

Make your positive connections whenever you can.

Connections are important, and remind you who you are, and what is important.

SOUL CLUSTERS

The people in your family were not chosen at random. You were born into your family for a reason. You were born into your soul cluster. Your soul cluster consists of the people you have been connected with in your past lives. Your husband could have been your father. Your child could have been your parent. Your friends, the people you are attracted to in your lives – they're also part of our soul cluster.

Maybe someone has done you wrong in a past life, and when you meet this person, you have an immediate reaction that is not good. But your family is your choice. You have chosen to be part of this group of souls, and this is the time to sit down and actually listen to what the people in your family are saying. Don't be afraid to listen to your husband, your wife, and your children instead of being absorbed in your own needs. As a family, you can support each other through talking, and through loving. Even if you can't have physical time with them, take some time to support those who mean a lot to you.

Allow yourself in this time – and beyond -- to do one good thing a day that makes you feel good. That's very important that you do one good thing every day. A good thing is a selfless thing – one that you do for no material gain other than the positive feeling you get deep inside. You all recognize that feeling, but so often you ignore it for the more material cravings you have. Do one good thing each day. That will feed your soul, and attract more positive energy and good things to you.

COVID-19 and THE BODY

Now, children of the earth, you must realize that viruses are connected with a chemical reaction. Some of these are man-made, produced by man, but some are produced by the souls of animals, in the time of the pigs and the birds. Too many of you have shown no respect for the animals. Only 5% of the human population respects the animals of the earth. You eat parts of them. They have a soul. That's not to say as humans you must not eat meat.

You must go back to the time before mass manufacturing of the meat. What you call the meat, we call the earthly souls of the animals. Back when you had to work very hard to capture your animal to eat, it was the animal's choice whether the animal gave up their soul to feed you. But now everything comes in abundance. Now you breed them so they're fatter. You breed them so they taste better. You tweak their DNA. You manipulate an entire species for your own glutton and desires.

Now, children of the earth, these animals were provided for their beauty to you, and yes, as a food source. But they used to have a free life, and their souls used to give up their lives on purpose to be eaten by you. They offered themselves as a gift. But now they have no choice. As babies, they're taken away from their mother when they're very young. The mother of the calf grieves for her calf. But you don't see this as they do not have a voice. The chickens go back to look for their eggs and wonder what's happened to them. Again, you don't see this as they have no voice.

COVID-19 started where it did with people who have little respect for the animal kingdom. COVID-19 was started by a chemical reaction between an animal's body and its consumption into the human gut. This began back in 2003, when a mutation of an animal part that was never meant to be eaten was taking into the human body, and mutated into a virus.

There was a cultural misbelief that certain animals, if they were captured, tortured, and eaten, would release a substance that would give people good health or everlasting youth. This is **not** true. If this was meant to happen, the animals would have given up their souls for you. But this is not what happened, and it is not right.

If you treat animals with cruelty, and then take them into your body, are you surprised that aspects of their suffering and misfortune will be taken on by you? The animals in the animal kingdom have experienced vast numbers of their own species being treated very poorly by you for your gluttony.

The Universe is now telling you that you don't need to do this. You have been given so much -- you don't need to be cruel to your animal species. It is your greed and desire to control the lives of animals in such an extreme way that has led to this situation.

In the later part of 2020 and in the beginning of 2021 and 2022, more outbursts of the virus will want to erupt. But this can be prevented if you all stick together and not allow it to happen.

Now is the time to ask yourselves – should you really inflict so much pain in your world? Should you not try to live in harmony with the other species of God's creations? Shouldn't you try to learn from each other, and enjoy together your limited time on the earth?

Your time on the earth is not very long but serves as an important learning grounds for your own personal learning curve. Your time on the earth is temporary so every worry that you will ever have is only temporary. But as a whole, we on the other side are very concerned about what you are doing to the earth. You are destroying the earth. You brought COVID-19 upon yourselves. You, as human beings, are experiencing a massive flock of your human lives ending. Although they're ending on the earth, their souls travel up to the spirit world, where we are greeting them. I must tell you, we are absolutely loving the souls we are receiving. Those who are dying of COVID-19 have chosen, just like the animals back in the day, to give up their souls for you to "feast" on them – for you to learn from their sacrifice. The souls that are no longer with you on the earth, that are dying from this COVID-19 are choosing to give up their lives so you can see what it is like for the animal kingdom to be losing their loved ones.

Every soul has a conscience. Some souls are more vast than others, and some souls are more in-tune. But every living creature that the Universal God has crated has a soul.

You would be wise to eat organically. If you eat meat, do it in moderation, and eat animals who have had a free-range existence and a chance to have a good life. Do not eat animals that have been kept in narrow confined boxes and cages. Avoid eating animals from big farms, where the space the animal is given is measured in inches or just a few feet –

formulas for mass profit. The souls of these animals are in pain. Ingesting this pain and suffering into your own body will not be good for you. Learn how the animal has been treated before you eat it – these things are not difficult for you to find out.

Some people chose to be vegetarians. This does not suit everyone. Admire your food and enjoy it, but choose wisely. Too much meat is not good for you. The hormones big farms induce into their animals to maximize their profits are not good for you. Let the animals roam and have a life. Let them have an organic free-range life. Do not let animals spend their entire lives as prisoners. They have done no wrong. Do not eat for the sake of eating, but choose your food wisely and enjoy it. Keep your food clean and natural, and you can avoid more problems in your food chain. The food chain is the source of your nourishment. Abuse it at your peril.

COVID-19 is the result of such abuse. It is a direct consequence of the inability of the human gut to absorb an animal protein never meant for human ingestion. This protein turned into a virus. COVID-19 reminds you that you are not indestructible. The destruction you have wrought on the animal kingdom has come back to you, through a chemical warfare. This was predicted by the late, great

Nostradamus. When you hear "chemical warfare," you think of guns and bombs. You've not considered a chemical reaction from the animal kingdom entering into the world of mankind. Now you see how simple it is for your species to be affected by a single virus in the food chain. You may have never considered this before, but the food chain affects you every single day. The choices you make *have consequences.*

In the past, the amount of energy you spent on acquiring food was very great. Now for many of you, food has become cheap. Still, many people starve, but your richer countries have more and more choices. In the rush to make food cheaper and more abundant for your richer members, quality has suffered. What kind of hormones and chemicals are in your food? What kind of hormones and chemicals are you feeding the babies growing inside you? As your children are born and grow older, they are given meat in abundance, and eggs in abundance. Is that meat free from artificially induced hormones? Are those eggs free of chemicals? Do they come from animals who have breathed clean air or do they come from creatures who have spent their entire lives stressed and abused?

You know that stress is not good for you. The protein from a stressed animal is also not good for you. It is not good for your soul. Now you see all too clearly the havoc it can wreak on your body.

There's no better way to understand the importance of a clean food chain then when it goes wrong. COVID-19 is a direct result of your species ignoring the warning signs. COVID-19 is your wake-up call. Ignore the need for a clean and respectful food chain at your peril.

The human race possesses the ingenuity to do many things. You have the power to overcome food-chain disease. You have the ability and the resources to make people sit up and take note. Many years ago, you were told through your tabloids that meat in abundance wasn't good for your health. But so many have chosen to ignore it. You have enough wheat and grain and vegetables which your Universal God has provided that taste so gorgeous, but you chose to go down the route of destruction of baby souls of the animal kingdom for your greed and pleasure.

Some of you ingest specific animal parts because you feel it gives you power. You crave the parts of animals going extinct because you feel this shows you are in control. This is not true. This is like a child who throws their toys out of the crib. It makes them feel in control, but leaves them with nothing. They learn nothing, and have to pay for their actions. You as a species are capable of so much more than this. Those who participate in the destruction of a species will be made to answer for their actions. Those who are cruel to animals will answer for their choices.

Not only do you destroy other species, some of you even sink so low as to destroy yourselves. Some human beings feel they gain power by drinking the blood of your own species. Some people eat the material of slaughtered embryonic infants. The terminations of babies that have been ingested by those who foolishly feel they are gaining long life and youthfulness – this is a grave mistake. All these people have done is absorbed the skin and flesh of a poor soul that has been murdered for greed. Whether that embryonic infant chose that to go to the spirit world on their own accord, their murder for the personal gain of another human hoping to steal more life for themselves cannot be denied. Those who engage in this will have to answer for their actions.

You want to know if there is a devil? This is 'devil worship' in one of its truest forms – to harm an embryonic human by ingesting it into your body in hopes of prolonged life. This is not only greed, it is foolishness. It will not make you live longer; it will put a stain on your soul that you will have to account for. This is something you will have to repay in some very real way.

Look at your leaders. You consider them your "higher beings" on earth, and you worship them in various ways. Maybe you look up to them for their power and fame. Many of your so-called "higher beings" are taking part in these deadly rituals. They feel that they're gaining power. But deep down it's an illusion, because when they will go to the spirit world they will have to account for their actions. Some may end up in everlasting confinement, unable to mingle with anyone else.

You who are on the earth at this time have been chosen to be there right now. You have chosen this for yourself. YOU have the power to make a big change in how humanity treats the earth and the souls that live upon it.

Child, the moon, the stars and the sun stay where they should be. They do not collide unless the Universal God allows this to happen. The moon is where it needs to be to give you light at night, while the sun is where it needs to be to give you warmth and light during the day. The other planets play their part with alignment of souls on the earth.

The God of the Universe is so strong that the stars and planets are as nothing. They are just a creation. You were also created. You were given the ability to enjoy the freedom of being an individual and experience your own life experiences. You may take enjoyment from singing, or dancing, or being a mother or a father or a doctor. So many choices are available to you. You are all on the earth to explore, develop, and enjoy your own special gifts. There's room on the earth plane for people to work in creative jobs, and a need for some people to be cleaners. Your world needs them both, the creators and the cleaners. Neither one is more important than the other. The souls of all humans are equally important. The soul of the worker with the lowliest job is no less important that the one who rules the nation.

The Universal God Spirit, what we call the everlasting life of freedom, is working very hard to allow your world to align again. You all have choices. This is what you were born to learn, that you have the choice to work for good or for greed in your world. You have the choice to help your parents or let them flounder when they age. You have the choice to help your friends or not help your friends. Being born human on your tiny rock that you call Earth, you have the freedom of expression. Some poor souls who were born with disabilities are there for you to learn from. If you treat these people kindly, your kindness will allow you to go into the next realm. If you treat the animal world kindly, you will go to a lovely realm.

There are many Realms of Heaven in the spirit world. This will be explained later. Know that your soul is immortal. What you do in your human life is the one thing you do take with you when you die.

I am very grateful that you are taking the time to listen to these words. And I'm grateful if you are considering how you could make a positive difference to the Earth and its inhabitants. There's an old prayer from many years ago that was proclaimed that you should <u>love each other like you all belong as one</u>. Unfortunately, we in the spirit world don't see enough of this happening. We do not see people loving other people equally. You are all part of the Universe and part of God's will. The Universe wants you to have the best life. The Universe wants your life on earth to make a positive difference. Learn with enthusiasm. Help with no hidden agendas.

And breathe. Breathing is very important. Breathing feeds the life-force that the Universal God has created for you, along with your heartbeat and your feelings and emotions. Your breaths are something that are each unique to you, and should not be taken lightly. You take your breaths for granted, as if you have an unlimited supply. You do not. The amount of breaths you will take in your lifetime is finite. Each one is an opportunity to engage with your earthly world in a special way – to take it into yourself. Do not waste the opportunity to appreciate your world as you take it into your lungs.

You will experience many different things leading through these troubling Armageddon years and you will have to stay strong. You will have temptation whether to stay on the good side or cross over into the bad side. The bad side is easier. The good side is more challenging, but remember -- the light always shines after the darkness is gone.

There will be a sign coming from above. The more you talk to your God, the easier it will be for you to recognize the signs. When you talk to the Universal God, speak to your God as you would to a friend. God doesn't want you to bow down and beg and say, "I beg you to make things different." Just talk to the Universal God as you would to your best friend. Tell God your fears, and let God fulfill you with the information your heart desires. Especially in these times of isolation, it is important to really talk to your Universal God. Really download your problems, but do not beg. God doesn't like begging. Talk to God as you would to a teacher or mentor. Speak to God yourself, without the filters of other people. Go deep inside your mind to where your spark of God light exists, and God will respond to you in abundance.

EMBRACE YOUR HUMANITY

Read your spiritual books if you choose, but remember – they have been altered over the years. The alterations do not serve you. Let's discuss the Bible. The Bible started off as a means of promoting law and order back in the ancient days. Laws were given to you to respect your fellow man and live in harmony. But huge parts of the Bible are now missing, particularly the parts where the prophets explained that you can speak to the Universal God directly, without the need to go through a church leader, or a rabbi, or a high priest. As humans, you have been given the ability to have direct communication with your Universal God. Do not let others with their own personal agendas try to corrupt this.

In this new era and the new world order, you must learn to be humane to other people, the animals, and everything that lives upon the earth. There's more darkness than you know that is coming. You must learn to take care of each other. Take care of the people that need to change, and help them understand. This is the dawning of a new age on the earth plane. You call it the earth plane. We call it the little rock that floats inside the Universe. To those of us in the spirit world, this little rock has caused us so much trouble. We are pleased that some of you are talking to us. Others choose to ignore us for their own greed and ego. They feel that man is all powerful, and they do not feel it important to speak to their God.

But there are a few of you talking to us, asking us to help make it right. We're not giving up on you earthly beings but make no mistake, my children. This is a time of Armageddon. This is the chemical war of your food chain.

By September 2020, you may decide the problems are swept away – "under the ocean" as you might say, but they are not. This chemical warfare that's been created through your food chain will be ongoing. It is a result of not having the proper respect. The people from the hierarchy that you call your nations' leaders are not really leading. They're destroying the planet. The service they are doing for you as your rulers is not serving you or your world. They are leading you into destruction in order for them to claim more greed for themselves.

But, my children of the world, we do not want this to happen. We are approaching the time where we need to step in. There are 144,000 chosen souls roaming the earth. These are what we call the peacemakers -- the beams of our light.

We have sent them to you to help you. You can join them and become a beam of light, too. Choose who you trust wisely. If you're not sure, meditate on it. Listen to the voice deep within your soul – the voice that tells you right from wrong. This will help you decide who to trust and when to be cautious.

RIGHT AND WRONG

You were given an innate sense of right and wrong. You were born with this. It is that voice deep inside you that knows the difference. You were also given intelligent reasoning to figure this out. You are consciously aware of the things make you feel bad, and you know that when you do these things to others, they will feel bad, too. You know that your ACTIONS HAVE CONSEQUENCES. This is the first thing you teach your children. Yet as adults, it's the first thing you like to forget.

To remind you how you should behave with your fellow humans, you have been given, through religious teachings, the basic laws from God. These involve respecting each other, not harming each other, and treating each other as you would wish to be treated. Still, all too often you go against all these things – your heart, your mind, your teachings from the spirit world, and your conscience.

Your "leaders" pit you against each other, then stand back and watch. You allow this. What are you thinking, my children? What are you doing to each other? What are you doing to yourselves? Those that do not respect life do not respect God. They do not respect the gift of life that's been given.

What do you think awaits a child who harms his brother? What awaits a child who disrespects her parent? You do not allow these things in your children, but as adults you give in to these things in yourselves. You make excuses for what you know in your heart is wrong.

Circumstances change, but ***you control what you do***. You control how you treat others. You control how much respect you have for each other and for yourselves. You control whether to listen to the voice within you that tells you right from wrong.

Listen to that voice. Follow it deep within your mind. Let it guide your actions. Let it lead you to the source of all joy – the oneness with your creator. From there, then shape your world.

GUIDANCE FROM THE HIGHER REALMS

Right now, in the spring of 2020, there are 11 works being dictated by us in the spirit world for you to know the truth. Many spirit guides are collaborating and helping to write these books. Of these works, this book will be the 3rd book to be released to you. These works are being sent to you now because this is an important time for the human race.

Some of these works will be written in other languages, including Hindi. There will be differences in the wording, and differences in the formats. But the underlying message of these works being dictated from the spirit world will be the same. That message is very simple -- that you are in control of your soul's destiny. You can converse directly with God. Do not let your ego get between you and your God. Do not allow someone else's ego to get between you and your God.

Some of you may not be allowed access to these works. The works may be withheld from you for political reasons. Some rulers may not wish their people to know they are not properly leading. Many of your world leaders are just puppets – dummy fronts with no substance behind them but their own greed. You have allowed them to be your anchor. Look to the right of them to see who or what is controlling them. Are they being controlled by money and greed and the lust for things that are not really needed? The innocence of children, the innocence of animals, and the innocence of your world has been sucked from your civilizations by the controlling side of so many of your so-called leaders.

There will be many other books written by people telling you what to do and what to think which do *not* come from the spirit world. Some of these books, including some presented by religious institutions and leaders, will be so far from the truth they are almost in their own realm, and not in a good way. They may be writing these books for their own power. They may be writing these books to gratify their personal egos or the status of their organizations. They may seem very convincing that they are doing this for a rightful purpose, or may truly be trying to help. But if they are not receiving their information from us in the spirit world, they are spreading false words.

How can you tell the difference between works that have truly been sent from the spirit world, and those that only claim to be so? Ask yourself this: where do they say the answers lie? If they tell you the answers are outside of yourself, to be held with another person or a specific organization with rules that you must obey, that is *not* correct. They want your power. If they tell you to obey their doctrine or your soul will face terrible consequences and damnation, that is *not* correct. They are trying to control you with fear. Do not let them do this.

If they tell you that *you* are in charge of your own soul's destiny, that is correct. If they tell you that you can speak to your God-force within yourself directly, without a mediator, that is correct. They may show you different ways and meditations to access your God spark deep within. They may give you methods to try that are different from the methods outlined for you in these pages. Different meditations might work for different people. However you access your inner God spark deep within, that is perfect.

As you approach September 2020, it will be a time that will seem peaceful after the summer. But let me tell you, around the month of December (2020) the problems will start to return again. Once again, innocent children will be abused for their youth.

Isolation is the time of rediscovering yourself. A time to ask yourself what you really want from your life. Where do you see your life going? How do you want your children's and your grandchildren's lives to be? The planets must stay aligned for this to happen, but the world is failing deeply. Imagine the worst scenario you can think of and times it by twenty. That is where your Earth is heading right now.

Some families will break up as a result of this so-called lockdown. Some families will not survive. Husband and wife may argue. Siblings may fall out. You're not used to spending so much time together. Go back to ancient times when all you needed was a cave – somewhere to shelter from the elements. Compare that with where your "gods" are now. Your leaders and influencers are showing you money and properties. The bigger the better. The most glamorous furniture. The grandest mansions.

But remember one thing. You do not need all this for your life soul to be happy. This is for pleasing your ego, and ego is NOT part of the spirit world. Your ego has no place in the higher realms. Your ego has no place in the Realms of Heaven.

You are not born with an ego. This is created. Ego has to do with greed and is fed by other people's greed, encouraging you to buy their possessions. Everything on the earth was made free. Your life was given to you for free. But on your world, everything has a cost -- where you live, how you live, and what you eat. You are enticed by things you do not need. You are coaxed to want more by the rich who are getting richer. Who are they to take from others when their most important possession – their soul – is given so freely?

Look up at the sky. Can you claim a star as your own? No. It does not belong to you. Nothing on earth truly belongs to you. You are only care-takers for the Earth for a very short time. Then someone else will be born and take your job, and on through the ages. Your part of that job will soon be gone. It will not be remembered. The most important thing to do with your life is to create peace with your Universal God. Your life is finite but your soul goes on. Know that if you create peace with your God, you will be equal to your God. This is powerful, indeed. This is **true** power.

There's also going to be a time, not so far away, that will be challenging. Children born in this era are going to be calmer than the children born in the last 50 centuries. In the past 50 years, people have been born with the determination to succeed and to gain material things. You believe you put a man on the moon. So you did. But what did they find? They found nothing but dust. You went diving through the sky and the heavens. You went straight through us but we chose you not to find us or our life-force.

As spirits, we exist in energy around your solar system. Yes, there is life on other planets but that is many, many galaxies away. You will not see these places until you reach the third Realm of Heaven. That will take your soul many life-times for you to achieve.

The Universe has got big things in store for your world if the earth returns back to normal. Families could again rejoice being together, and everyone could be equal. The so-called leaders and the people who are leading them who are full of lust and greed will find things very different when their lives are over and they reach the Heavenly Realms. The people will not be rewarded but will go into their own personal Armageddon.

We are so sorry you are experiencing this pandemic, but we could not let the earth continue on the way that it was going.

Take care of your soul. Your soul is your internal life-force that carries you on from this world to the next. Maybe you will return again if there is a world to return to.

We need to raise the vibration of your world everywhere. You can help with this, through meditation. You live in a vibration bubble of energy. It is important to keep the vibration energy up, and keep it positive. Everyone is scared right now and the Universal God is not receiving positive vibrations from the earth.

You are now feeling scared for your loved ones and your own health and your own mortality. But remember – your life was never going to be anything but temporary. Your soul is what matters. Your soul is pure energy.

The Universe is made up of energy. The way the stars stay up in the sky, the way the moon shines above you -- everything around you on the Earth is made up of energy. Right now you must tell the world and the animals and the plants that you love the world and you love being part of this bigger picture. You must heal yourselves and the earth. You must remember why this has happened, and learn to really appreciate everything you have been given.

The generations after you will need to take care of the Earth as well. You want them to inherit a beautiful planet, with rejoicing, and beautiful music and films. You want the Universal God to be pleased and love your planet.

The Universal God is a united energy field. People may call it God, or Allah, or many other names. As conscious spirits of the world, you must give out your love to the Universe. You can do this through meditation or prayer. Remove yourself from the fear and the anger that has been bred by this COVID -19. Breathe in and out deeply, allowing all the toxic and negative thoughts to drift away. Allow yourself to connect through your energy with the higher creative force of the Universe.

I would like you to picture in your imagination how you would like your world to be. How you would like the animals in the future to be? How you would like your family and friends to be? Resist the urge to focus on the negative. Understand that you are being shown how it feels to be cooped up for a reason. The lockdown of isolation is very much like being in a very confined zoo. You are like caged animals, controlled by your so-called leaders and the ones who control them. This is how you treat so many of your animals – locked up with no ability to escape. You will eventually emerge from your zoo, but many animals that you confine in crowded spaces will never have that chance.

The 144,000 of you who are spiritually guided will outshine the rest. Pure energy and pure love are what the earth needs. The Universe will assist them and a little light of hope will shine through. You can join them and help. You can add your positive meditations to the voice of positive vibration. But the energy around your world right now is very dark. It needs to have more light shone on it. It needs encouragement. With the pure goodness of your hearts, look at why this is happening and look at where you see the future heading.

Don't look at this time as being only negative. Humanity has been through many dark situations on the earth. You've been through famine and wars. You've been through politics, and assassins but this pandemic is hitting hard because it is stretching into every corner of your little planet. People in Africa, people in America, people in New Zealand, people in England -- people in every continent are hearing about this and feeling the concern and fear.

This pandemic affects your whole world, not just individual countries. I ask that you, as a spiritual energy being, release the positive energy that you have inside you. Do what you can to dismiss the negative. Do what you can to commune directly with your God. Do what you can to raise the positive vibrations of the energy inside you radiating out.

The conscience of the Universal God is all around you. Pull it close to your chest. Love this energy field of positivity. Create your destiny and the destiny of mankind. COVID-19 is a chemical reaction to your bodies – it does not affect your soul.

I am being drawn to remind you of what you call the dark side. Now, many of you know on this earth that you have some very dark souls walking among you. These dark souls portray a false beam of the light of excellence. They hide behind their power and wealth. They hide behind people of the cloth. They hide behind doctors, they hide behind performers, film directors, TV presenters, and people of sports. Not all these people have dark souls. Some of these souls are pure love and light. But the ones with dark souls can be so magnetic and flashy that they can attract you. They can blind you to their greed. Once they impress you, they have touched you, and you have allowed them into your own soul. You may love the way they act or how they look on TV, and you may follow them to get more of their programs. You might like the way they play football or cricket.

You may love your doctor because you've learned to be respectful of people who are going to help you. But so many people, even people of the cloth in their temples of diamonds and money and control, can attract people to them for the wrong reasons. People are attracted to loud and glittering people who promise spiritual rewards.

These people are offering something they have no ability to give. They have no right to promise such things. Forgiveness is something humans crave. These controlling people understand that very well. They offer forgiveness if you heed their doctrines. But why would you think you can get forgiveness from an earthly being? How can they offer forgiveness to you when they have their own humanly lessons to learn? Why would you feel the need to pray in a place of worship that has so many riches that those in charge could feed all the people of the earth for the next 200 years?

These riches of organized religions are things they have taken from the earth -- from the planet. Everything in your home is taken from your planet. People might create, but the resources have to be taken from the earth in order to be created.

Let me tell you, children of the earth, these false people with their false idols and greed can rise so high in the public light. Many of you look to them for guidance. Many of you allow these dark ones to control you. They control many bad things, including the abuse of young children and the abuse of animals. Life is not enough for them. They want power.

But their 'power' and their 'light' and their selfish energy field will fade. When the creator calls them back to be nothing but a soul, their souls will go into everlasting darkness, and their lights will not shine anymore.

Be wary of people who promise you favors with the Universal God if you follow what they say. You must ask yourself – are they really trying to help you, or are they trying to help themselves? You cannot buy your way into harmony with the Universal God with money, or favors, or the number of humans attracted to you. The way to God is there for each of you, and it is much simpler than you may think.

You must know that your souls have been put on earth during this time for a reason. You are there to embrace the God light within, and become a speck of light between the areas of darkness. You don't have a strong voice yet as there are so few of you, and you are not powerful right now. Just like the animals in the zoo, you have nothing but hope. Cling to that hope, my children. Through meditation and groups of meditation with other like-minded souls, release that positive love you carry inside you. Let it flow from you, and spread. The world is thirsty for the power of this love. You can't see it. You can't touch it or taste it. But just like the love that you have for people who are dear to you, you only have to feel it deep inside to know how real and how very special it is.

RESTORING EARTH'S BALANCE

Every few thousands of years, even hundreds of years, even every few tens of years, it is necessary to restore the balance on the Earth. It's a shift of consciousness to enable you to reach higher moral grounds. These are times you have to shed your fear and go with your deeper thoughts to your higher conscience. You need to achieve balance on the earth. The sooner you find balance, the better your human society and the rest of the natural world will be.

For too long, the balance has been ignored. You thought you had conquered disease. You thought you were so great that you did not need God. You believed in the power of your own fragile mortal bodies instead of the strength of your everlasting souls. Now your world has become so unbalanced that unprecedented actions must take place. As humans you are destroying the earth and your planet is dying because of the result of your greed. This is why now you need to look deep within. You need to access your higher conscience and restore the balance.

You need to ask yourselves what do you really need. Look at the mountains upon your land. What do they really need?

Look at all the species that live amongst you. You are taking them for granted and allowing yourselves to not pay attention to the inner truth of their lives. Instead of appreciating the beauty of the earth, you look at how to change things, to satisfy your greed.

Restoring balance is necessary. Look at your highest conscience, without any greed, and explore what you find beautiful about your lives. What you need to think about is why you are here on this earth. You are here to learn, and to nurture. You are the care-takers of what you call Earth. You are here at this critical time to put the balance back in. You need to examine why things have been done for greed and gluttony, and how to avoid these mistakes in the future. You need to look at the highest truth inside you. You need to consider your natural existence and the beauty of the world around it. Until you take a long hard look at these things, and learn to make positive choices, there will be no balance on earth. The destruction will continue until it is too late to stop it.

Right now you are going through a learning re-curve. The destruction happening to the Earth now could not continue without dire consequences. This pandemic is only one of those consequences. This is a wake-up call. Now is the time to learn or re-learn what must happen in order for your world to continue on.

Everyone was plodding along in their own little bubble, but now those bubbles are burst. A part of your world is dying, along with many other species. A portion of your people are dying, because the balance has tipped to dangerous proportions. There have been man-made things inserted into your food system which you are not supposed to be eating and are causing diseases inside the human body. The human body was not built for this. Yes, drink your wine, and yes, drink your beer. But all the man-made chemicals you are ingesting are causing a natural disaster for your bodies that can spread to your soul.

Everything in God's garden was meant to nourish your bodies, in moderation. Anything processed by man to get rich by greed is not good for you. Spirits are crying out for the suffering you are causing for the poor creatures in your rivers and on your land. You are ignoring their cries and feeling it is okay to destroy them. But remember – your actions have consequences. Disrespect and destruction have consequences. Your job is to respect the world you have been given. Destroy it and you fail, not only for your species now, but in the future.

Why are you here now? Are you the ones who are to save your world? The answer is YES. The problems compounded by many centuries must come to an end. Worshiping in gold-plated churches will be coming to an end. You are to know that you can worship your God on your own. Each one of you has the same connection to the Universal God. Nurture your own personal relationship with your Universal God. You don't need to seek out men with fancy robes. Establish your own connection knowing that God is inside you. God is part of you.

Understanding this balance is necessary for humans to make the world a better place. This is your last chance to gain balance before we, from above, will be forced to interfere so much that your world will no longer be. The acceleration of your climate change, spurned by your need to travel on a daily basis is not doing your world any good. You need to explore the truth of why you need what you think you need – and need and need and need.

This increasing cycle of need is encouraged by your hierarchy. Your car manufactures and airplane companies and your leaders give you the feeling that you've got to go more places and have more things. Yes, you may travel the world freely. But do not do it to be selfish. Do it for the love of your soul and not for the greed of your mind. The Earth was created with the perfect conditions to sustain life. This was done for your benefit. Balance and harmony with your animal kingdom and your garden that God has provided can be achieved. But you must be at one with your Universal God, and you must grow deeply and spiritually.

You must do what you can to make a difference. Look around you. There are small things you can do. How good do you feel when you help someone unconditionally? How good do you feel offering small acts of kindness? Hold on to that feeling. Do what you can to enjoy that feeling, through your good actions, and your positive communication with your Universal God.

You don't question that you are breathing the air. Similarly, you don't need to question that God is part of you. To be good caretakers of the earth, you need to become as one with the Universal God. You don't have to give up your religion. Some people find that their religion helps keep them spiritual. But know this -- you don't need a church or a mosque or a temple to find God. Go to the peace inside your own soul. That's where you truly find God.

Talk to the Universe. Tell the Universe what you want. No matter how you talk to your God, you are talking to the Universe. Do a universal prayer every day, if you can. You can say things like, ***"Thank you for my life. Thank you for the souls around me. Thank you for the lessons I've learned. Bring me the lovely lessons that I'm capable of learning."*** You can say what you are trying to achieve that day or that month or that year.

If you enjoy the community spirit of church or the temple, by all means go. As human beings, you are born to share in communities. Even before you had houses, you had communities. Being amongst like-minded people you can feel a community connection.

But don't just listen blindly to the person preaching to you. Do not think you can recite someone else's words and be done. You don't achieve real communication by reading off of a script. Go deep within yourself and connect directly with the Universal God. That is your right. Do not let someone else pray for you. They can't speak to your God for you. You must do that for yourself.

RELIGION

Religion comes from the day when we in the spirit world needed to create law and order for you in the physical world. Even as early as the first human beings who set foot on your land, we could see there were problems with some humans wanting control over the others. For that reason, we had to send down laws for you. You call it religion. We call it the ***laws of humanity***.

There are many religions. Religion has had a positive part to play, and many religions have positive messages for humanity. From the Buddhist views of peace and harmony, to the off-springs of Christianity and the Muslim and Hindu and Sikh religions, religions have played a very honest part in your communities. They have allowed the commandments of the ***laws of humanity*** to be given to you. However, it saddens us that through individual greed and power, religions have been used to allow certain humans to gain power. Whether it is emotional power, sexual power, or monetary power, the religions of the world have been compromised by the greed of some of their leaders for control. Sometimes humans have added their own laws to religions. Some have added that the man can have several wives, or that the woman has no freedom unless her husband allows it.

These ideas did not come from the Universal God, they have come from humans wanting power over other humans. As human beings you have allowed these ideas to creep into your religions.

Religions are not sacred. Many started from teachings given to you by those in the Heavens. But over the years they have been changed and altered. Although there may still remain important messages within them that have been allowed to remain, parts of them been corrupted to drain your souls of your true life's purpose.

I tell you to go to your prayers and pray to the Universal God. Speak directly to God. You do not need to go through a religious leader, especially one who tells that you are somehow less than they are. Be cautious about giving your power to someone who wants it this badly. Why do they feel a need to take your ability to speak to your God directly from you? What are they offering you, and why? What do they get in return? What do they gain by creating a block between you and the Universal God who made you? Why do they feel they are more special than you?

Do not give away your power to connect with your God directly. This was given to you by the Universal God. No one has the right to take it away from you. If someone tells you that they are the way to God, be cautious, my children. The right to speak directly to the Universal God was given to each of you. Any human person or organization who tells you to relinquish that right and give it over to them is misleading you. No earthly being has the right to restrict your direct connection and communication with your Universal God who created you.

The benefits of the good things you do in life outweigh the bad things. Sometimes you may feel that you do good but never get anything back. That is because society has caused this, and sometimes rewards the wrong things. You must always do good because every good deed has a positive effect. Even small acts of generosity are important. Even a small thing as saying hello to someone who might not have family or friends – such small things can make a big difference in your world. They can make a big difference to your soul.

If there is a dog in the street who needs a home, take it home and give it a feast. If a child has no shoes and you have extra shoes at home, give them shoes. You do not have to give brand-new things, but you must give with a pure heart. The benefits of giving will come back to you. The Universal God looks upon giving with great respect. As humans everyone has been made equal. The lions in the jungle, they have a ruler but all are equal. All the dogs are made equal. Even your possessions are made equal.

Look at your TVs. They're all the same. Your mobile phones – they come in different models and makes, but all are the same. Some are bigger, some are more colorful, but such things are surficial. You are addicted to having "the best." You have been programmed to crave and want what is new and flashy, even if you do not need the new features. Be mindful of what you truly "need." Do not let your "need" of having more and more material things crowd out your joy in giving, which is where your true joy comes from.

PRAYER

When you connect to the Universe, talk to the Universal God as if you are one. Whether God is a singular consciousness or multiple consciousnesses, it does not matter. God is energy and energy has no number. Be free to thank the Universe, as a friend, for the life you have been provided with. The greatest gift you possess is life. This lifetime you are in now is a relatively short time in your soul's existence, so you must appreciate it and use it wisely. Your life-force is your breath, your heartbeat, your mind, and your soul. Your life-force is everything that you are that matters.

Remember when you connect with the Universe, to be appreciative for what you have been given. Don't say "God, do this for me and I will shout from the hilltops about you." No. Just become one with God and accept that God has already provided you with the blessing of life. Whether you call the universal life-force God or Muhammad or Jack Smith, it doesn't matter. God is the great creator of the Universe. Look around at the stars and the clouds. This has all been created for you. This has been engineered to allow you to gain and sustain life.

When you connect with God, relinquish your ego. Try to pray every day. But don't pray as if God is a superior being that judges you. You must pray knowing God is inside you, on a friendly level. Do not shout out, "God, please give me money. If you give me money, I will talk about you and tell everyone about you." God does not trade favors for promotion. Just say "Thank you, Lord for providing me with what you have so I can live and breathe." If you want to travel, that's okay. You can say, "Thank you for my life, and allowing me to go India to see these lovely souls there."

The way you talk to your God and your Universe is important. Leave your ego out of it. Don't say, "Look what I've done for you today. See how I rescued that old woman." Instead, say, "I've done something good today that has made my soul feel blessed and nurtured me by doing it. Thank you for the strength to do good things, and the wonderful feeling it gave me." Enjoy that positive emotion of feeling blessed and nurtured by doing good deeds.

If you speak to God with an appreciative and generous heart, it is very easy to talk to the Universal God without an ego. It is important to become one with your creator. If you don't, you will miss out on a wonderful opportunity that you have right now, every moment of your life. This is the power to connect deeply and personally with the Universal God, and establish a powerful relationship that will sustain you well beyond your lifetime.

For too long, you have been wrapped up in an increasingly materialistic world. Your actual needs are much simpler. You need water, food, and pleasant souls to be around. You don't need all the consumer things you think you do. You have a saying "the one with the most toys wins." This is so foolish, yet many of you believe it, to some extent. You find yourselves engaging more and more with objects and things. This creates a desire for even more things. You have lost much of the ability to integrate into societies of people. You have lost the community spirit. Now you live so individually that the community spirit has gone. This leads to boredom, and all too often, you try to appease that boredom with even more things.

There are positive ways to deal with boredom. Nurture your creative spirit. Paint, draw, sing, perform – enjoy the simple pleasures of your life and your world. If you are unable to engage physically with your community, there are many ways to connect with the spirit inside you. Society wants you to look at the adverts and hunger for the next best thing out there and strive for it. But that will lead you down a path that will not satisfy you. That has been created to satisfy someone else's power. Allow yourself the freedom to remove your own ego when you pray deeply with the Universal God. Allow yourself to be full of gratitude and appreciation for the many blessings you have been given.

When you remove your ego from the inner conversation, this will allow you to truly connect with the Universal God, without creating the barriers of your human greed and desires. There is a feeling of peace and harmony that comes when you allow yourself to link in with the Universal God in this way. *This deep internal connection is your right.* It is right to feed your soul with this inner connection. The Universe is your friend and the Universal God is friends with you. It is that simple.

This is a sample of how the Universal God likes to receive your prayers. This is the kind of dialogue your God likes to hear from you.

Dear Universe, thank you for my life. Dear Universe, thank you for the lives of my family and my friends. Dear Universe, thank you for the life of every human being that is on the earth. Thank you for all the souls you have provided in the animal kingdom for our pure pleasure to look at. Thank you, Universe, for the mountains and the sea and for the grass and the trees. I thank you, Universe, for making me feel good, and giving me the ability to feel and the ability to love. I thank you, Universe, for everything I have learned and everything I'm about to learn, as I truly believe that this will be provided to me. Thank you, Universe, for my children and for the life of my grandchildren and my great-great grandchildren in the future.

It is important to thank your God. The Universal God wants to you be thankful and appreciative of all you've been given. Give to God your thanks for the ability to be on this earth plane and for everything you are learning. Give thanks for your soul and the other souls you meet and can learn from.

Sometimes you may feel very enclosed in your own little world. Remember the importance of community spirit. The rules from God are to love each other and thank each other for your souls. Your soul must learn to be accepting and loving. Every day, thank your God for your life and for everything you've achieved in a positive light.

But put your ego aside. Your true achievements are not of your ego, they are the positive feelings within your when you connect with your true inner spirit. Your true achievements include the positive energy you have contributed to the souls around you. Do not be deceived by the ego of others. Someone with great ego may have great wealth, and seem to have great power, but this is not real power. This is a temporary power that will turn to just as much dust as their bones will.

All too often you take your life on earth for granted. It might seem simple, that you have been given life on earth. However, consider the forces and complexity that it took for you, as a living sentient being, to be afforded life with such a high level of physical ability and self-awareness of your soul. The chances for self-aware and conscious life are astronomically and statistically improbable, yet here you are.

Early in mankind's history, when you were back in the caves, you needed to rely on each other. Community spirit was strong. In today's world, you have lost the immediacy of that community spirit. Issues of ego have crept in. You have forgotten the simplest of God's rules – to love each other. You have lost respect for each other, and in doing so, you disrespect yourselves and your creator. You are to love and appreciate each other. You are to thank your fellow humans for their souls, and realize your souls are connected. Every day of your life is a gift. Every soul you connect with is a gift.

Every day is an opportunity to engage with the Universe, and be thankful for that gift. Each day you should be grateful. It takes very little time to say, **"Thank you for my life and everything I have achieved. And thank you for allowing my soul to develop and thank you for keeping us safe."**

This is a simple thing to do, and it will not take up much time. Yet this simple thing is so important to keep connected with your God, and in the right way -- with appreciation and gratitude.

You are children of the Universal God. You are all equal as you are all made in the same image. Many religions will tell you that you are made in God's image and this is true, to an extent. But this is not a physical image, as God does not exist in a physical form. God is pure energy, and energy has no physical face. Think of a radio wave. It has no legs, and no beard. But it has the power to carry great knowledge. Your God's energy also has no physical presence, but is so much greater.

You were born in God's image in that you were created with a spark of God light within you. With this spark, you can connect and commune with God whenever you wish. This is a powerful gift. But you are still learners. You are still like children.

If an earthly child says, "Can I please have that?" and responds with a "Thank you," this shows respect and love. However, the parent does not appreciate it if the child says, "Give me this. I want it now." This doesn't demonstrate respect.

You must talk to God with the same respect a parent deserves. Just like you were tied to the mother's womb as you learned to grow inside her, you are tied to the Universal God's life force as your soul develops in the world in this lifetime, and then beyond.

Think of all the things that went into creating your body. Think of all the things that went into breathing life into your soul. This was no small feat. But all too often, you take the miracle of your life for granted. When you pray, do not ask for things that feed your ego. Those are the thoughts of a greedy child. Engage with your creator with thanks and appreciation, as you would want your own children to engage with you.

The prayers you should say should express your gratitude. For example, you could say, "Thank you, Universe, for getting rid of COVID-19." It won't be the humans who get rid of COVID-19, it will be God's will whether it will happen or not. Don't pray with need and conditions. Don't say, "God, give me this and I will shout your praise to the hills." You pray to a God that is equally beside you.

It is important to be truthful about the things that you want. Do not be greedy with material things, but you can use prayer to bring about the future you wish for yourself that would nurture your soul. It's important to feed your soul so you can help take care of others. If you are achieving, you can be an example for others.

Here is how you should pray. You should **not** say, "Oh, God, I need this or that. Please give me money and I'll be your best friend forever." God is not a "prize" to be doled out to those who demand things. But God is there to listen to you, and wants you to succeed.

You can say, "Thank you, Universe, for my life. I am receiving love in abundance. I am loving my new home. I am blessed to be a loving person. I am blessed with all the gifts you have given me and all the things I can do. I am blessed to be [[a mother, a father, a teacher, a musician, a driver – all the multitude of things you are and are able to do]]. I am blessed to be me. I am blessed that my God has given me creation, and that part of my God dwells within me."

Whatever your heart desires, pray as if you already have it. The perfection of the miracle of life granted to you makes you worthy. As you pray, channel the divine energy of God, and trust that what you desire to feed your soul will be provided.

The sun doesn't drop in the cosmos. The sun accepts that it was put there at the creator's wish, to do what it does – to give warmth to the Earth. Just as the sun was put there for a reason, so were you. You don't exist as a result of pure chance, you were created to live your life, enjoy it, and learn from it. It is no accident that you exist. Every cell of your body is perfect. Every part of you works together in the wonderful dance of life. You must not only express your thanks, but express your joy in the gifts that you have been given, and appreciation that your gifts are perfect in God's eyes.

If you are an artist, know that your art is beautiful in your creator's eyes. If you are an accountant, know that your honest work is beautiful in God's eyes. You deserve to do well in your life, because you were blessed with so many gifts. Speak to God in your prayers as if you have already achieved what your heart desires. This shows that you trust God, and God appreciates your trust.

Think of the times when you reach deep within to that place inside you that offers you a connection with the Universal God. When you reach that place, there is a sense of harmony and peace. Do you know this place? If you don't, search inside to find it. It is there inside each of you. This, my children, is a reflection of God's energy. This reflection is within you. You were born with that spark of God's energy within you, which you can access at any time you want to feel your creator's love. This allows you to connect, anytime you wish, because it was put inside your soul.

DIFFERENT TYPES OF SOULS

Humans and animals have souls. Your souls are alive but your bodies are dead. Your soul is your connection with your higher self. Your soul is your energy, your thoughts, and your feelings. Your soul carries you on through many different lives on Earth and your soul is eager to learn and be learned. Animals have souls as they share much of genetic makeup with you human beings. They need to be respected as beings with souls.

As for your bugs and worms and creatures that live underground, they all have tiny souls. Their souls are not on the same soul-plane as yourselves. They will learn different things for their soul growth. When a person dies and their soul comes back, it will only come back into another human body. A dog's soul will only come back into a dog's body.

As for the dinosaurs in the prehistoric eras, they had souls, too. Once they went extinct, their souls came back as other creatures. The Universe is full of dinosaur souls. You will see those souls in your fishes and other creatures. These souls are older than your human souls.

You have chosen to be on the earth at this time. The animals in the animal kingdom also choose to be on the earth at this time with you humans so you can learn from each other.

The plants are there to sustain life for your energy. The plants and trees do not have souls like you, but they have a life-force that allows your souls to have life on earth. They are there to provide for you and the animals. While the plants exist with you, their life-force belongs to a different realm. But your journeys are there on the Earthly plane together. You all chose to come to the earth together at this time. Remember that. Your soul may have qualities an animal's soul can't conceive, but they came here for you. You can learn from them. You must learn from them or one of your precious opportunities to learn will have been wasted. Your life will have been wasted.

Plants do not mind being eaten. They have no feelings and no consciousness. They are there for you to enjoy their beauty, provide materials, and to be your food.

OTHER SOULS AMONG YOU

The heart of the Universe is energy. Your heartbeat, your brain force, and everything in the Universe is all held up by energy and that energy is God. The Universe is expanding before your eyes. The energy is getting bigger and bigger. As human souls, you cannot comprehend how big and how fast the Universe is. There is no start and no beginning and no ending of the Universe. Planets far away look at your little planet and wonder what's going on. Many times, you have been visited by what you call aliens. We call them other planet caretakers. They try to come and show you what is right and wrong. However, you humans have such ego that you cannot look at anybody else's point of view. No other souls hold power, only yourselves, so you believe.

However, you have aliens walking around you right now. You remain unaware of their presence. They're on a different vibration to yourselves. Your eyes can not see their matter. Your souls cannot feel their souls as they vibrate at a different level. Yet these souls have chosen to leave their comfortable planet many light years away, to come and walk beside you on this earth plane to help you. Unfortunately, your egos are so vast that you can't accept what you can't see.

Humanity is not the end-all and be-all of existence. It is just one part. Your present life on earth is only a small part of your soul's journey. Just because you can't see something doesn't mean it doesn't exist. You can't see the energy of the Universe, but you know it's there. You can't see the power that holds the sun and moon in place, but it's there.

Most of you humans have very little trust and faith. You think "faith" is blindly believing in someone who has a religious degree. This is what you value.

This comes from years of conditioning. But know this -- the light people that walk beside you are trying to shine some light of energy onto you. They want you to see more clearly how your world could end up if you don't make a change. Know that others are giving of themselves to try to help you. Let that encourage you in your journey to seek a higher spirituality. Be comforted by this and let this help you find your way.

DIMENSIONS

We spirit guides and helpers in the spirit world are tied to the Universal God, too. There are many realms, and they are expanding more and more. You on the Earth are in the third dimension. This is a learning dimension. This is a dimension of consciousness. I have been told by the Universal God many times that your position on the Earth, within the third dimension, is a favorable position. You are not on the top, or the bottom of the levels of dimensions. There are those in dimensions more and advanced, and those in dimensions less advanced.

These other dimensions don't really affect you. You exist within your own dimension. Look around at your world. See how it is fragile and perfect and beautiful. Embrace the beauty around you.

Then look within. Access your God-light within. There is beauty here, too. There is power and grace and so much more, all deep within you.

THE REALMS OF HEAVEN

As human beings, you are very inquisitive. You don't like being told what to do. You're learning this difficult lesson right now as you deal with isolation. While this is hard, it is a chance to go inside yourselves. Ask yourselves -- what makes you scared? Are you afraid of what God can do to you? You are taught that if you're bad, you will go to hell. If you're good, you are told you will go to the heavens. This is not entirely true. But if your soul is worthy, it will be allowed to continue on to higher realms. If it is not worthy, it will not progress.

There are many higher realms – many heavens. But there is only one Earth.

You humans will have at least 11 earthly lives to learn the lessons needed for your soul's growth. These lessons center around issues of humanity. In general, this involves being kind, being understanding, not being judgmental of others. It involves keeping your ego in check and never letting it be your guide. There are more specific lessons that an individual soul may face, and an example of that will be given later. For now, know that the big lessons focus on humanitarian issues – loving and caring for others as you would wish for yourself.

If a soul requires more than 11 lifetimes to learn, they can have as many lifetimes and earthly experiences as they need.

There are many realms but not all of these are available to you. For you dwellers of Earth, there are seven heavenly realms available to you. Some religions, including Islam, Judaism, and Hinduism have already told you this. The energy of these different realms is located around your solar system. These spiritual realms are your seven Realms of Heaven. Upon death (termination of the body) your soul will go to one of these realms where your consciousness will meet your creator, the Universal God.

You don't get to choose which realm you will go to. You will be sent to the level of the realm that your spirit has achieved. You will be guided there by the arc-angels. These are spirits charged with ensuring that your soul winds up in the correct realm.

These seven realms are represented by different colors, and different planets. As your spirit evolves throughout your various lifetimes, your goal is to progress up through the level of realms, to higher and higher levels of spirituality. The seven realms, going from the lowest to the highest, are as follows.

1. The first realm is the blue realm. The energy of this realm is near your Moon. Correlating the Realms of Heaven with various celestial bodies will help you visualize the order of the realms. This first realm is the lowest realm that a soul would travel to upon leaving the earth plane. It is the least-evolved realm spiritually.
2. The second realm is the silver realm, represented by the planet Mercury.
3. The third realm is the purple realm. The energy of this realm is around your planet Venus. For most souls, it will take many lifetimes to achieve this level.
4. The fourth realm is the red realm, represented by the Sun.
5. The fifth realm is the orange realm, represented by the planet Mars.
6. The sixth realm is the green realm, represented by the planet Jupiter.
7. The seventh realm is the gold realm, represented by the planet Saturn. This realm is also known as Quran.

The more advanced your soul becomes, the higher up it will go in these realms. If you have been godly in all your 11 lives and have done nothing wrong, upon the end of your 11th life, you would go straight up to the gold realm. This is actually very rare.

If you have not learned very much, and your soul needs help, you will be sent to the first realm, the blue realm. If you have been very bad in your lifetime, you will be contained in a learning center in this first realm. You will not be allowed to leave the learning center until you understand and accept that you have done wrong, and are sorry for your wrong-doing. There will be spirits counseling you and trying to heal your soul. Their job is to help you acknowledge your mistakes. Some souls will embrace the learning process and repent. From there, they will be sent back to the earth to work through their wrongful ways in their next lifetime(s). What they achieve spiritually in their very next lifetime will determine which realm they ascend to once that life is over.

But some of these damaged souls in the blue realms learning centers will refuse to learn. These souls will remain in these learning centers, unable to leave or move on until they accept their wrong-doing and wish to become better. It may be that they never learn. If so, they will remain there indefinitely, not allowed to mingle with other consciousnesses. They will not be allowed to harm anyone else. But they will not be destroyed. There will always be room in God's heart for them somewhere, and these learning centers on the first realm of heaven is that place.

There is no "hell." Your God is a loving God and would not create such a place. But a soul trapped in its own selfishness and the memories of their wrongful ways with no desire to do better is an existence devoid of joy. Being trapped forever, alone, in one's evil memories and selfishness is as close to "hell" as could be imagined.

The lower the realm you arrive at upon death, the more likely you will be sent back to earth. Your soul will go through at least 11 lives, but it may require many more before it no longer has to return to a physical life on earth. It may need 50 lifetimes before it leans enough to progress higher.

If you are sent to the first three realms, you will need to go back to the earth for further learning. Your soul will have been deemed needing further growth.

When you come back to the earth plane, you will not know what you have come back for. Your soul has to come back fresh and eager, and willing to learn and gain knowledge. But if you come back and ignore your higher conscience and do bad things, once your soul returns to the Realms of Heaven, it will go to a lower realm. It may even go to a lower realm than what you had previously achieved.

Your soul's energy is pure vibration. Your soul can vibrate with a good energy if you've done no wrong in your life. If you have done bad things like murder or abuse, your soul will vibrate with a bad energy. Remember – ***thought goes where the energy is, and energy goes where the thought is.***

Once your soul has achieved the level of the fourth realm, you will have learned the important lessons and you will no longer be required to return to earth for another life. However, you may wish to go back for another earthly lifetime to be an ambassador for a humanitarian reason. You may wish to return to Earth to protect children, or animals, or some other meaningful goal. You may also wish to come back for another lifetime with the souls in your soul cluster to help them learn their lessons.

The higher up in the realms that you go, the more choices you will have. In the spirit world, you may wish to become a helper or a healer or a messenger. You may wish to help shape other worlds and other realms. There are many choices you will have in the upper realms.

In the fifth realm, you will not have to return to the earth, but as with the fourth realm, you may choose to come back to earth for a particular reason which would benefit the Earth.

Angels are spirits that have never lived on the earth. Angles are heaven's keepers – souls that have never had human lives. There are angels in all the realms, but there are more angels and arc-angels in the 6th and 7th realms. The 6th realm, in particular, has many angels.

By the time you reach the sixth realm, you will no longer go back to earth. Your earthly experiences and the memories of those lifetimes will no longer matter, and will start to fade away.

When you reach the 7th realm, you will be in complete compatibility with the Universal God. All souls are part of God, but upon achieving the 7th realm, you will be more entwined with holiness than you will have ever been on any other realm. You will lose all memories of your past human lives as your experiences will have served the purpose of your soul's development, and are no longer needed.

While the main lessons for soul growth and development involve humanitarian issues, there are specific things a particular soul might have to learn. For example, one human father, during a lifetime, witnessed the death of all four of his children. Of all the many lives this soul had experienced, this was the most difficult experience of all. It was so hard that this father could not accept that there was a reason his children were taken from him. He spent the rest of that lifetime unable to accept the loss. Upon his death, this father ascended to a lower realm, and had to come back in another earthly lifetime to learn that there was and is a reason for what happened. He had to understand there was a reason for these deaths both for the growth of his own soul and the growth of the souls of his children. This father's soul had to lose the bitterness of that loss and accept the higher purpose in order to evolve and progress. In his next human lifetime, this soul also lost a child, but learned to accept it. Upon completion of that lifetime, this soul ascended to the fourth realm, and no longer had to return to an earthly life.

In other parts of the Universe, other self-aware and conscious beings are progressing up the spiritual realms around their worlds. Some of these various beings are progressing at a much quicker pace than you on the earthly plane. One particular species is learning their lessons and becoming at peace. So many of their beings are achieving their 7th Heavenly Realm. These beings are many years away from you, and a million years ahead.

Why are other these beings progressing so much faster than your human soul development? For one thing, their world is much older than yours. They have already spent many lifetimes going back and forth from their Heavenly Realms to their lifetimes on their physical world. Over time, they have learned to make wiser choices in selecting their leaders. They do not suffer the consequences of following damaged but charismatic leaders like your Hitlers.

Look at the sky when you go up in an airplane. You go high. In the clouds you can't see the earth below, but you know it's there. What is above you? Planets and stars? What's beyond them? You can't see it all, because it is not your time yet to touch those realms.

As humans, you are inquisitive, and this is good if used rightly. The Heavenly Realms are important, but there are other realms, too. New realms are being created all the time. Just know that there are no beginnings and no ends.

FREE WILL

You were given free will on the earth to be in charge of your destiny. This is your choice. You were born into your current life to learn certain things. Only when you step away from what you have to learn do you feel unloved.

This is when some people in their lifetime on earth feel they don't belong on the earth and decide to end their end days. They cannot cope. They cannot learn the lesson. Upon their death, they will go to the first realm – the blue realm -- and have to come back again to learn what they should have learned before they did the crime of taking their own life.

Upon their death, their soul will arrive in the first realm and they will be asked by the angels, "Why did you do this? Why did you feel you could not cope? Who hurt you so badly that you decided to take your own life? Who abused you? Who took your power?" Not only will you be judged if you do this, but other people who contributed to this will also be held in judgment of this.

There is no hell. Hell is not something that exists for you. Hell is a man-made idea. Hell means fire and loneliness, and is a concept created by the hierarchy (your human leaders) to keep you fearful of your true God. God is a loving God. The Universe is loving. Do you feel that the Universal God would make such a place? The answer is NO. If such a place existed, do not feel for one minute your creator would put you there.

DEATH

The biggest fear that a human has is death. You were not born with this fear, but society has created this for you. The fear of failure, the fear of being run over, the fear of airplanes – these fears have been created by society and your own mind. It draws me back to when people in ancient days used fear to control. There is no better way to scare a human being than through the word "death." Even the fear of death can be enough to make a person die.

In truth, death is not the worst thing that can happen to you. Death WILL happen to you. The worst think that could happen to you would be to die WITHOUT establishing a personal relationship with the Universal God. The worst thing would be to not have a loving relationship with the Universe. The worst thing is entrapment in the physical world.

When you die, you leave your matter behind and become only energy. You transform from your physical body into your spiritual body. Look at an ice cube. It starts off as ice, then water, and then it evaporates. One form changes into another. Nothing is lost, it merely shifts form. Your body is not needed in the other realm. What is needed in the other realm is your soul, which is your conscience. What is happening on earth now during this pandemic is that everyone is running about with this fear of death.

Death is not to be feared. After this period of time on your little rock, things will have to change. You will have to stand united, you true believers in the heavenly realms, and ask your questions. Why do you need to feel afraid? Abide by the basic law of the Universe which were written in the texts such as the Bible or the book of Koran. The basic laws are very simple. You mustn't kill. You mustn't thieve. You mustn't hurt animals or children. You must respect life. These are basic rules. These are the things you must pay attention to.

So many religions have been cluttered by additional rules. These "religious rules" that have been handed down to you have been molded and shaped to suit the egoistic part of mankind, not to suit you.

What I am telling you is that on this earth plane, it's not the virus you are afraid of, it is the word "death." When you hear the word "death," you are going to be fearful. What the hierarchy like to do is to keep you fearful and needy. In that way you can be controlled.

As a society you can remove yourself from a consumer market. You can remove yourself from having the biggest house or the best car, or working every hour under the sun for this illusion that you have created something. Yes, you will have material possessions, but your soul has cried out, "Oh, God, please, I wish I never had all this pressure on me." But you don't change it, you carry on in your striving for "perfection."

On the other hand, you could turn your back on society's creations and focus on the beautiful birds and bees. Focus on your modest little house with your modest belongings. As long as you've got food in your belly, water to drink, and shelter from the elements of the world, then you as human beings can survive.

Do you really need that fancy TV? Do you really need that new mobile phone? These are "needs" that have been created for you. You fear you're not hearing the television so you will miss the news. You fear not having the mobile phone in case of emergency.

But one thing I can tell you. When it's time for you to leave your little planet and come further in the heavens, you may realize that what you have striven for was not really worth it. If you look at what you've achieved on the personal and spiritual level, you may realize you have achieved nothing. You may realize you were too busy getting your new car, or going on your next world cruise, or looking at your money in the bank.

But if you have come here to embrace your life's lessons, then these can be taken as needed, endured, and learned. In the meantime, you can create some good karma. You could look at animal protection. How good would that make you feel? Saving a child who has nothing, how good would that make you feel? Helping another family have dinner – how would that make you feel?

Remember these things, because after you die, you will be asked to account for your life. If you heed this advice, when you're floating into the heavens and the Universe asks you, "What did you do with your life?" you can reply, "I loved my life because I was really happy. I achieved things that helped others, and I am happy that I gave."

As human beings, your fear is failure, and your fear is death. With those two fears installed in you, the hierarchy will always have control over you.

But remember, when you pass away and join us in the other realms, if you worked your whole life for nothing but material things, you will realize you can't take an ounce of it with you.

SPIRIT GUIDES

Spirit guides dwell in the Realms of Heaven. We have chosen to help and guide you. We were once human, too, and have already gone through our multiple lifetimes. Because of that, many of us initially came from ancient times, particularly the first kingdom of ancient Egypt. This was an especially powerful period in human history. Egyptian civilization was quite advanced for its time, as we had to deal with many things, including the alien "bird-men of the skies" and the death of our king. In the centuries since, many of us who lived in ancient Egypt have progressed to the point where we no longer have to return to the earth. This has left us free to become your spirit guides and helpers. Other spirit guides who lived on Earth in other times are also assisting me in delivering these messages to you.

Each person on Earth has at least one spirit guide. We silently guide you, but we do not directly interfere. That would interfere with your free will.

You can meet your spirit guide through guided meditation. A sample of a guided meditation follows. The ability to travel to the Realms of Heaven, even while you possess a human life, is one of the many powers you possess within your mind.

A GUIDED MEDITATION TO THE HIGHER REALMS

To make the world a better place, humans must learn to work with the Universal God. You must learn to ask your questions and form a direct connection to the Universal God. This is a beautiful energy. Your soul needs this. Your world needs this. We in the spirit world are just starting to see this happening. Now is the time for this shift before it's too late for your world.

The power of your mind is so much greater than you realize. You can use it to take a journey into the higher realms now, while you are still alive. Here is a guided meditation you can use to take yourself there, into a higher realm where you will be absolutely engorged in a loving light, the universal light of God. This is a meditation you can use to channel the Universal God, the Universe of love. You can use it to meet with your spirit guides and your loved ones who are in the heavens above you.

To do this, you can record the passages below for yourself to listen to, and meditate on. Record it in a calm and peaceful voice. Then find a quiet place where you won't be interrupted. Lay yourself down, and breathe.

Take a deep breath in. Breathe in all the beautiful energy of the Universe. Breathe in through the nose. Now breathe out all the toxic thoughts. In through the nose and out through the mouth. With each breath, you are feeling lighter and lighter. Protect yourself with a beautiful bright wand. Use this wand to put a cloak of protection around you. You can say the word "abracadabra" or any other word you chose to make your wand form a cloak of protection around you.

Feel yourself very rooted. Get some imaginary twine and root yourself, your root chakra, to the floor or the bed.

Keep breathing and breathing. Visualize a beautiful rowing boat. As you walk towards this boat, you are feeling very tranquil and very relaxed. You sit yourself on this lovely wooden rowing boat. As you are sitting there, you start tapping your third eye. Your third eye is your spirit eye -- your connection eye. It's right between your two eyes, just above your nose. Keep tapping it and visualize it opening up. This will allow you to see very clearly on your journey.

As you tap on your third eye, you feel calm and relaxed. You can feel the sun beating on your shoulders and on your back and you are feeling very loved.

As your little rowing boat starts heading row down the river you come across a big oak tree. On this tree you see faces – faces of your loved ones that are no longer on this earth plane. You see the faces of your spirit guides. You will see faces of people you have never known in this lifetime. Spend some time telling the tree of spirit your problems. Unload your fear. Unload the fear that you carry with you.

Spend some time really talking to the Universe that is connected through the oak tree. Ask the faces and the Universe to protect you and to help you. You start to see things very clearly. Allow yourself the power that you need in order to be a positive citizen of the earth. Draw in this special strength.

Spend some time in lovely conversation and feel the love of the Universe. Ten seconds or an hour, it's up to you. Spend the time feeling the Universe and the energy around you. Feel the tingling all over, like a cobweb tingling on your nose. Absorb yourself with this feeling, so you feel the pure energy of the Universe.

When you feel ready to carry on with your journey you can feel your rowboat going up a steep, steep mountain river. It's almost like gravity is pulling you up and not down, and you feel yourself being pulled into a different realm.

As your rowing boat evens out into the river, you can feel that Mother Earth is a long way away. But you're feeling very safe and you're feeling very loved by the Universe.

In the distance you can see a beautiful island. As you approach the island you can notice figures of people and animals on the island. Your boat draws up to a southern port and you get off your boat. And there beside you stands your spirit guide. Turn around to face your spirit guide. Ask them their name. Ask them all your questions about your life that you're experiencing on the earth. You can ask them, "When will I pass away?" "Where will I be going then?" "What do I need to learn?" Ask them all the questions you would like to know. Feel the purity of the answers in your own mind. Remember that your first thought is from spirit, and the second thought is from your own mind – your own ego.

As you turn around there's a big banquet where there are many chairs, and many energies sitting on the chairs. Your guide walks you around and pulls out a chair. You sit and you embark in conversation with the people at the table. But please do not eat or drink when offered as you are not part of that realm right now.

Spend as long as you want asking questions, and really store it in your conscious or subconscious mind. Ask it to be stored where you can bring it up in the forefront of your mind later on, when you need it.

Your guide comes back around and guides you back to your boat. Your guide gives you an object. Remember that this object is given to you from your spirit guide. As you look to the right you see an animal. This is your power animal. This animal is your protector.

You thank your guide for allowing you time in this realm. Then you go floating down the stream. As you start coming back to Mother Earth, you're feeling that you're falling, but you're very safe.

As you hit the earthly part of the river, you know you're back on the earthly plane. As you go past the oak tree, you wave to the energies on the spirit tree and thank them for the knowledge that you've gained through them. As you come back to the earth and back to the river bank, you are wide awake. You are feeling calm and you've obtained all the knowledge in your subconscious. It is there, inside you, whenever you want it.

GUIDED MEDITATION THROUGH THE ASTRAL PLANE

Back in ancient times, people used to induce a sort of near-death state, for their souls to leave the confines of earth and become free to explore other realms. They used to take hallucinogenic drugs that allowed the person to have an out-of-body experience. The kings and pharaohs and even Jesus himself took this drug, which was plant-based. This allowed the soul to travel and leave the earthly body, and engage with the Universe. This has been called astral planing or astral projecting. Astral projecting is an experience that takes the soul to a place where the consciousness is so pure that you can be anything or anyone. There are no battles of will. You can become one with whatever you desire. It is a death of ego.

Although the plant that was used to produce this hallucinogenic state grows naturally, it can be dangerous and is now illegal to take. For some people, it can open up the third eye so wide that they may completely lose touch with the physical world. If this happens a soul may not have the strength or will to return to the body. This can result in the destruction of the brain, or it can cause true death of the body. This is a sad outcome as it leaves their loved-ones on Earth mourning for them for leaving before their time.

However, we've allowed your human mind to have the ability to break down the barriers for this to happen naturally, without chemical inducement. You no longer need this dangerous and generally illegal plant to achieve this experience. Now we are now allowing the human brain to access this experience of the systematic death of ego, and reach this state without drugs, through meditation. [1]

The ego death is something that is self-induced -- something that you have to seek out. It allows you to leave the depth of the earth behind and look beyond it. Social barriers break down – you will not be controlled by the media or by your world leaders. You will see things differently, and clearly, through the third eye – the spiritual "eye" that exists in all humans.

Things that used to bother you, including thoughts of negativity, will go. You will start to feel very positive. You will become very much in control of your life.

---

[1] Editor's Note: This sounds like something called "Holotropic Breathing."

If you look at the drawings on the pyramids, you will see that the pharaohs were connected with life on other planets and brought back certain knowledge. The God of the Universe allows this but it must be done with complete and utter understanding that your soul will enter a different realm. You will feel the freedom of the Universe. Everything that was around you will no longer be there. Through the death of the ego, you will experience a connection with the Universe. Many of your leaders and spiritual gurus have known this secret. They have practiced it behind closed doors to gain superior knowledge. Some of them have tried to use this knowledge to control you.

Now that astral-planing can happen through pure meditation, gone are the days when you have to take a plant-based substance to enter into the different realms.

What follows is a guided meditation for you to explore calming your mind in order to achieve this state. You may want to record the following passages in a calm, peaceful voice, for you to listen to and meditate on if you wish to practice seeking a journey through the astral plane.

Sit down and relax. Close your eyes and breath very clearly, in and out. With every breath in, you are breathing

in positivity. With every breath out, you are breathing out negativity. As you are being very much in control of your breathing, put a very strong imaginary rope around your ankles – a lovely rope keeping you very much tied to the earthly plane and attached to your physical body.

With every breath, feel yourself becoming lighter and lighter. Feel yourself floating. Pay attention to the peaceful sound of these words. As you feel yourself floating, feel yourself very calm and very tranquil. Feel your surroundings of peace. All your negative thoughts are drifting away. As you drift towards your ceiling, it opens the roof of your home and you start floating above the building that you call home.

Embrace the energy around you. Feel your creator's love that's inside you. As you are breathing, you can feel a magnetic force that is pulling you up.

If you are feeling scared at this time, you can ask to be returned to your physical body. If not, carry on with your journey. It doesn't matter if you get this far four or five times before you chose to extend further. That is your choice. But if you do decide to extend further, you can feel yourself being pulled up like a vacuum into the heavens.

Note that I say "heavens" since there are many upper realms. However, there is only one Earth.

As you feel yourself floating, you are feeling very warm and very tranquil. Look at your lovely earth that you leave behind as you soul continues on your journey. With every breath you take, you go further and further into the heavens.

Then you come to the astral plane. This is the plane where you can ask your purpose. You can be anyone or anything you want to be. You can ask the Universe what the next level is above you. You can ask about God the creator. You can speak to God the creator. You do not have to remember what answers you receive – that knowledge you will gain will be stored in your subconscious, to be retrieved whenever you wish. It will be stored for you, for after come back from your journey, you will find yourself more knowledgeable and more spiritually-awakened.

Now that you are within the astral-plane, look around you. What embraces you is the conscience of God. Feel all the connectivity around God and the force of being at one with your maker. Your energy combines with God – you are one with your creator. Ask your questions, seek your answers. Or just be.

I would like to take you up into further realms, but this is something you will have to do with a guru or spiritual teacher physically present to guide you.

Now I want you to breathe, and feel yourself being pulled back into your earthly body. Enjoy the experience of returning to your earthly body. Feel your earthly body. Feel the miracle of life within you. Give thanks for all the blessings that you have been given, and all the blessings to come. Remember that feeling of deep and everlasting love that your creator has for you. Keep that in your mind and your heart as you engage once again with your world on the physical plane.

This is one way to meditate to travel on a journey to achieve a higher conscience. This may not happen right away. You may not achieve the astral-plane of your higher conscience on your first try. But through determination and clearing of your mind, you can allow yourself to experience the ego death. You can experience the cessation of your ego and leave it behind to become one with the Universe.

As mentioned earlier, the pharaohs of ancient Egypt did partake in journeys to the astral plane. If you take the time to study the technology that the pharaohs had, you may be surprised. They had the knowledge of brain surgery, when the western European cultures were living in mud huts. Look at the Aztecs. They had similar drawings to those found in the pyramids because there were also connecting strongly with the different dimensions of the Universe. We have put the chemical in your brain, so with true faith and true determination, you can do this. It is a temporary death of the ego, and not of your soul or your physical body.

If you do not reach the astral plane through your meditation, do not be discouraged. It may be harder for some to let go of their physical state. Know that you do not need to reach the astral plane to engage in a dialog of gratitude and thanks with your creator. It may be that your path is to engage in other patterns of self-awareness and positive connectivity. Simple meditative dialogue with your creator may provide you with what you need.

Keep meditating, and on a regular basis. The benefits of continued meditation cannot be underestimated. Through meditation and going deep within your mind, you can communicate directly with your creator.

Through group meditation, this is how you can join with other like-minded souls to create a more positive world. This is how you can combine with other souls to raise the vibration energy being put out into your world.

If all this was not enough to convince you of the importance of meditation, know that your scientists are just now "discovering" the powerful and numerous benefits that deep, repeated meditation has on the human brain, the body, and mental health.

THE CHANGING FACE OF RELIGION

Back in 300 A.D., the Bible was edited to fit in with what the leaders of the time wanted the normal people to fear. They took away the sacred truths and added fear so people wouldn't ask questions. The Universe and God became separated, but I remind you that the Universe and God are the same. Whatever you want to call your God, God is at one inside you.

It is hard for you as humans to understand this because from a very early age you are told that God – Muhammad – Buddha, whatever you wish to call God -- is a separate entity. You have been told this to separate you from your God. You have been told this to give power to those who wish to put themselves between you and your God. The truth is that the only church you must follow is the church inside yourselves. God dwells inside you. Listen to that special place deep inside you, with gratitude and a giving heart filled with love. That is where you will find your God. What you learn from there is what you must follow.

In this time of separation, the church and your leaders are telling you what to do. There are indeed things you can do in order to protect others, and doing what you can to protect others demonstrates care and respect.

But it is also important to remember that *you are souls in a material body*. COVID-19 cannot harm your soul.

Let's go back to when Jesus was chosen to deliver messages. He said, "You are powerful, and deep inside you is the knowledge." Those were great words, but they have been lost. They were removed from all records for a reason. This reason was not for your benefit. You have been led to think of God as a separate entity, with a separate "house" where your religious leaders work.

But now is a time to reflect and receive new messages from us in the spirit world. It is time to learn and understand that you and God are one. Never let anyone tell you to fear God. Do not give them your power.

God is like the parent, and you are like the child. Would you allow your brother to speak to your mother for you, and never speak to her yourself? Would you fear that your mother would banish you to flames if you didn't follow your brother's rules? Of course not. Do you think God loves you any less than you love your own children? Of course not.

The time to regain your God-given power to commune with your creator is *now*. The time to rekindle that spark of God light within you is *now*. *Now* is the time to nourish your inner light, and let it shine.

THE NATURE OF GOD

The rules God sent down to Earth for you earthly beings long ago were set with positive morals. They were channeled through mankind to keep law and order on the land. They were given to you to tell you that God walks not just among you but inside you. God, the great beginning and the end, has given you a means of direct communication and wishes to commune with you, the chosen children. God wishes you to learn and achieve your soul's growth.

God tells you, "Ask and you will be given." In these times of trouble, why not feel the loving God inside you and become friends with your God? Many times I've been asked, "Is there more than one God?" The answer is yes, and no. Yes, because you are all gods with your own power. You all carry a spark of God's light within you. But there's only one entity that travels the entire Universe. Yet this one entity walks inside each of you.

Back in Egypt there were scripts that would give you the power of understanding. But the leaders of the world refused to put these passages in your western Bible. These scripts told you not to fear God. They told you how to commune with your God.

But men wanted that power. They wanted you to bow down to them, and to force you to come to them to reach God. This is not the truth. Believe in your God and God will believe in you. God is neither male nor female; God is pure energy, and energy has no gender.

Look at the Gnostic teachings. The Gnostic works have documented many things, but these teachings are now hard to find.

Let's talk about Satan, the Devil. It was proclaimed that he was cast out of the Heavens and that he walks around you on the earth. I will tell you that no loving God would cast away one of his angels. The devil is not around you. You can act like a devil yourself because you are privileged to have your own thoughts and feelings. You have been told if you don't follow certain rules you will be stuck in isolation with the devil, but this is a form of control, propagated by other humans seeking control over you. Remember one thing – there are many people on the earth and many souls in the spirit world above. There are many people who can act like devils. But there is only one Universal God.

In this time of isolation, fear not. As you are looking inside your own soul, look deep. The soul that you possess in your material body will someday leave this earth and go to a different realm. Do remember that you must be kind and good and treat people the way you want to be treated yourself. These things are important. Unlike material things, these are the things you will take with you when your cross over to the other side.

The ten commandments were put into place to guide you. They fit into everyone's life. If you abide by most of these rules, you will be doing very well. Just remember that God is a loving God, and God is inside you all.

LIVING A POSITIVE LIFE

What should you do every day, every week, every month, and every year? You should look at the person you really are. You should consider the person you want to be spiritually, and search for ways to achieve that. Every day look in the mirror and find something you like about yourself. You are God's creation and there is much good about you. Look into your writings. Look into the things that make you feel you are a beautiful spiritual being, inside and out.

Look at nature in rain, snow, and in all weather conditions. Appreciate mother nature. Look at the sea, if you're close to the sea. Look at the forest, if you're close to the forest. Think of the wild life that lives in this environment. Spend some time sitting in a quiet place there and meditate. There's nothing better than meditating when you're grounded on Mother Earth's soil.

You should take time every day to pray, and connect with the spirit of God within you. This is your time to be grateful for the opportunity to live another day on the learning plane of Earth.

At least once a month you should take the time to nurture the creativity within your soul. You could write or sing and spend time with friends. Socialize, and start building up a community spirit inside your friend circle. But also, once a month, it's time to really reflect on your life's journey. Ask your spirit guides questions with every new month, about the path you should take within that new month. Ask what this new month holds for you, and what you should bring to it. Ask what your life's pathway should be. Do not be afraid to ask many questions.

Once every year, you need to be grateful to the Universe that you've had the pleasure of having another year on the earth. Celebrate your birthday not with only the traditional things, but with the joy that you have been given an entire year of new experiences, and opportunities to learn and grow.

As spirits, we don't have the same sense of time so it's hard for us to comprehend the timing of you human beings. Your body will die, this is certain. With COVID-19 you are reminded of this frequently, and you worry about why and how and when and if. Take precautions to protect yourself and those around you, but take away the fear and use this time to reflect. Reflect on how beautiful the earth is now and how beautiful it could be. How much of a difference can you make to make it better? Choose a focus and start there. Just as you might decorate your house once a year, help decorate the Universe with caring and kindness. As the Universe loves the earth, this is how much we love the Universe.

This is a time for being grateful. This is a time to take nothing for granted. Every day wake up and be grateful. You have been given another day. Talk to the spirits like they are your friends, because they are your friends. The Universe is your biggest friend. It has no beginning and no end. Remember how small your little rock is, and remember that the Universe remembers. Whether the Universe is one consciousness or many, this does not matter. What matters is **the Universe knows you**. You cannot hide who you are from your God.

Once a year, at least, thank the Universe for providing you with another year in your physical body. Do not disrespect this gift but keep it as strong and vibrant as you can. When you leave this earth plane, you will leave it behind and go to another realm. There is no death of spirit, only the death of the physical.

Sometimes the transition beyond death is easy and the soul has no trouble making it to the other side. But sometimes it is difficult. Remember to have a kind soul and the Universe will be kind to you.

SIGNS AND SEERS

Over the centuries, humans have had an urge to know what will happen. Many cultures through history have embraced seers for this. Only a few thousand of the truly gifted seers can make correct predictions. You can seek them out if you wish.

Nostradamus predicted many things. He predicted a major war "when pigs fly." People thought this was nonsense, and ever since, the phrase has been used by you on earth for ridicule. But during World War I, the pilots wore masks of pig leather. Watchful eyes looked out from behind the skin of pigs to oversee the bomb runs and the dogfights in the air. Nostradamus also predicted World War II and even the name of Hitler except for one letter. The Twin Towers was also foretold. There have been many signs.

Jesus was one of the important prophets sent to you. If you would like to know more, look to the old testament. There is great wisdom and important teachings there. The new testament also has some wisdom and teachings, but this part of the bible has been more altered by mankind for specific purposes.

Muhammad was another great prophet sent to you. Muhammad predicted many things in the future. Through his connection with the Universal God, he was also able to see into the past how the Universe collided in order for the planet earth to fall within the exact parameters required to sustain life. The Miracles of Quran are unique among the works of the prophets for their scale and scope.

It was foretold to you many years ago that 2020 was going to deliver Armageddon. Many feared that Armageddon would involve God with a big bolt of lightning coming down and striking you. But Armageddon has many forms. There were signs that pandemic was coming but you chose to ignore them. Society tells you to ignore the warnings. Your culture says, "How could someone know this in advance?" But it was very much there in black and white. If you knew that the realms were connected, it opens up the Universe of psychic connections. Your hierarchy didn't want that. They didn't want you to know.

A passage was added to the Bible that states, "Don't seek a fortune teller." It warns that if you do, you will rot in hell. This was added because your leaders do not want you to know what they are up to. They don't want you to be able to channel this amazing energy for yourself. They put "the fear of God" up you, not for your benefit but so you will give your power over to these power-hungry men. There are charlatans in every field, and the areas of politics and religion are no exception.

What I tell you is to seek your true seers. Find the ones who can communicate with us in the spirit world. Seek these true seers as the messengers between your two realms. Seek them to see beyond your realm to help you understand the larger picture. If you can do this, you would not be so willing to give over your money and possessions to be controlled by people who sound convincing but want to control you to feed their own egos.

Predictions are being made now by people on your world who do not truly understand. The predictions made by so many of your government officials are operating on ego. You have to consider the source. Are their intentions true and genuine, or do they have something to gain?

By January 2021 your lives will be somewhat back to normal. You will be thinking, "My God, what happened?" You should be thinking, "My God, do not allow us to go back to that, we've learned our lessons." But you can foretell that your hierarchy – those in positions of power -- will take the credit and reward and golden glory for what they have achieved to get rid of the virus.

I tell you to ask the Universe. Speak to your God. If we wanted the virus to go away, we would have made it gone by now. The virus will be walking around you for many years as a silent killer until you have learned what you need to be learning. Respect your animals and respect your fellow humans. Respect the planet you call Earth. Respect your God by communing directly, and in an appreciative way. In this way you respect your life and your own selves.

We are all energy. It is held between us and within us – the energy of healing, self-healing, and the energy of your soul. Your heart-beat is made up of beating energy. Every cell of your body produces energy. Your muscles produce an energy. Rise above, you chosen flock, and see the grace of God inside you. Stand tall and stand alert or others will try to control you and make you do things that would harm your soul.

MANIFEST YOUR FUTURE

Seers use different tools to aid them. Tarot cards, runes, dousing, crystal balls, pendulums, palm reading, astrology, numerology – these things can help a seer understand what the Universe is trying to show them. These things can assist the translation from the pure energy we send down to you, to the thoughts and words and images the seer receives. Today, being in control of your own destiny has become more openly discussed and more valued. In this pandemic of 2020, people thirst for answers. Go within to look for answers. Many of these answers you can find yourself.

If you need help, find a true seer. A medium clairvoyant can help you find answers to your questions. But as you have free will, the future is not cast in concrete. You can change the outcome by your course of actions.

When you go for a reading, be aware that the clairvoyant will not tell you what you want to hear but what they see. Be open to the process. Spirit will guide you at the right time when you need a reading, or when your higher conscience might want to know more. Go with an open mind, and go with strong specific questions. You can write your questions down on a piece of paper. You can do this in advance of the reading and can sleep with your list under your pillow beforehand. In this way you can manifest your questions to receive your answers.

Do not be afraid to be specific. Do not be afraid to help manifest the future you wish for. For example, you could ask, "Will I meet my future soul mate? In what month will I meet my future soul mate?" In this way, you not only ask your questions, but you help to manifest the destiny that you want from the spirit world.

But phrase your language appropriately. Do not say, "I want to buy a beautiful house." No one appreciates someone with needy demands. "Want" is a needy quality. Instead, frame your heart's desires with the language of trust. Say, "I will buy a beautiful house to take care of my family. Where will I buy it? When will I buy it?" Trust that the Universe will provide for you. In this way, you are working with the Universe, not coming with the expectation that you are not deserving and that the Universe will let you down.

Live your desire in your mind before it happens. Let yourself embrace it in your dreams. Feel it, sense it, breathe it, love it. Feel the warmth and the feeling of contentment. Now it's already there. It's already part of you. This will attract it to you. The Universe values positive action that is taken with good intent. The Universe values appreciation and trust from its children.

One of the most important messages you need to learn is that ***you are powerful***. You have as much right and as much power as any human soul on the earth. Use your power, and use it kindly.

TAROT

Tarot is a particularly useful tool of the seer. With these cards, you can also read yourself.

To understand the history of tarot cards, you must go back over 2,500 years ago. In ancient Egypt, it was foretold that the great Egyptian civilization would end up in dust and ruins, and their language would be forgotten. The masters decided that to preserve their culture, they created what they felt were the most important 78 images of their culture and painted these on dried animal skins. Each of these 78 images became a different "card" in the Tarot collection. These symbols were used by the seers, which at that time were called sages, to make specific predictions.

These "cards" became widely known, and traveled all the way into the far east. Other cultures took these cards and re-did the "deck" to remove the high priestess and queen cards, as they felt women were not "worthy." The Tarot deck went from 78 to 52 cards. The Chinese invented paper, and put the female cards back in.

From there, the first European country to embrace the cards was Italy. They were first used as gaming cards, but someone discovered they could be used for fortune-telling.

The "traveler culture", those who used to be called gypsies, traveled from India into Eastern Europe and used imagery from all previous cultures. They put their own spin on the Tarot images.

The important things about the Tarot cards is that they represent the different things going on around a person.

There is a specific type of reading called THE WILL OF LIFE reading. This type of reading will tell you the past, the present, the driving force, the way forward, and then a final overview. This builds up a complete picture of someone's life and can be a helpful guidance tool for someone with questions about their life's path. If you choose to have a Tarot reading, choose your reader wisely. Do not be impressed that a reader has "been on TV." Some of those seers are genuine, but some are not.

How can you tell a true seer from one who is not? Again, go deep within your mind. Meditate on it. Beforehand, see how you feel about them. What does your intuition tell you?

Afterwards, consult with your higher conscience and see if what they have said rings true.

Note that Tarot can not only help you see what may come, but can also give your warnings of things to avoid. You may meet a lovely new person and find yourself attracted very quickly. But the Tarot might give you a warning that this person might have a hidden agenda, and perhaps is not who or what they seem to be. Be aware that a reading sees not only the good but also things to avoid.

THE SEER WITHIN YOU

You can use the Tarot Cards or other tools of the seer yourself to perform your own readings on your life's path. This not only provides you a reading, but it also nurtures the development and growth of your own clairvoyant abilities. Some people are particularly gifted with strong clairvoyant abilities, but each person is born with some degree of clairvoyance. This is part of your subconscious mind. As I have explained before, your subconscious is connected to your physical body but also encompasses your soul which is somewhere between your physical body and the first realm of heaven.

Your cultures do not always encourage development of the gifts of clairvoyance. Children who express their abilities are often discouraged. Like a muscle, if it is not used, it will diminish. But it is not gone forever. You can work with a seer who provides guidance on developing your own abilities, and bring your own gifts to light.

YOUR PERSONAL RELATIONSHIP WITH GOD

You as humans on the earthly plane have a thirst to know your God. You were given a soul that seeks to know your creator, who dwells deep within you. You have been given time on your little rock, to learn many things and to nurture your soul. Religions have been given to you as laws to live with your fellow humans. Religions were created for the reasons they needed at the time, and the *laws of humanity* they imparted will always be important.

I have said some of these things to you before, but they are so important that you need to hear them in this way. God is your Universe and your Universe is God. It doesn't matter what you call your God. You were born with an innate sense of right and wrong inside you. Use it! But sometimes you ignore your sense of right and wrong. Like children who are learning, you have needed guidance. Teachings have been given to you, that you call religion. These include the basic laws, about respecting others as your respect yourselves. You are to love others as you love yourselves. You are to love the Universal God who created you as you love yourselves.

You were given the basic *laws of humanity* about treating others as you wish to be treated. But over the years, people have learned to corrupt religions. Selfish people have learned to harness the natural human desire to know your God, and have used this against you.

Heed the *laws of humanity*. If you ignore these basic laws, you are not being wise, and you will pay.

When these laws were given to you, there were fewer people on the earth and you did no harm to it as you walked upon it. Now you are many, and your way of life has become more complex, requiring more and more of the earth's resources.

Be careful how much you take. Take only what you need. The animal kingdom is already being devastated. So many species are going extinct right before your eyes. Some species will be gone forever. Some species will have horrible short lives, bred only to feed your greed. They will never breathe fresh air or walk freely or know kindness.

COVID-19 is a wake-up call. It is a reminder that your time on earth is precious. It is a reminder that what you do to your world will come back to you. Now the world is giving you back what you wrought. You have abused the animal kingdom and this is the result. You have abused your blue waters, and you will reap the price of that. Your hierarchy – your worldly leaders – work hard for their own gain, to feed their egos. This makes them appear great, but that is an illusion.

Now in this time of crisis, we of the spirit world give you new laws to add to the basic laws. Yes, respect your fellow humans as you respect yourselves. That is important. Yes, respect your God, the provider of all things. That is vital. But respect the animal kingdom, too. Respect your planet. Know that its resources are finite and will run out if you continue to abuse them.

Now that you have time to reflect, it is time to remind you of the important things that have been removed from your religions. The most knowledge is that **you have the power within your mind.** You are to USE this power. DEVELOP it. Follow where it leads you. Let it help you feed your soul. Let it help you heal your world.

This power is within you. It is not in someone else. It is not in a religious "leader" who wants to control you. It is not in a list of rules dictated by someone seeking power. It is around you and within you. It is **deep within the mind.**

Go there, deep inside your mind. Go there often and freely. This is your right. This is your need. This is where you can fulfill that deep desire to know your God. This is where you can speak to your God and learn the truth of your life's purpose.

Give of your heart. Give often and freely. Do one good thing every day.

Use your time on the earth wisely. Do what you can to make the earth a better place. Do what you can to make your community a better place.

Be cautious of those who wish to control you for their own greed. This diminishes your power to do good. This diminishes the growth of your soul.

Do not be seduced by other humans who offer you heaven if you do certain things for them. Many terrible things have been done by those promising rewards in heaven, and this makes us very sad. Another human being does not have the power to determine where you will go when you die. Know that your body *will* eventually die, and when this happens, your soul *will* travel to one of the heavenly realms. This is certain.

But if you allow someone else to get between you and your God, and you heed their rules without question, you will have learned very little. Your opportunity for personal growth will have been wasted. Your lifetime will have been wasted, and you will have to come back from the heavens to live another life on earth in order to learn what you were meant to.

If you allow someone else to take a test for you, will you have learned anything? Of course not. It is the same with your spiritual growth. If you blindly follow someone who tells you they have all the answers, and you accept all their doctrine because they speak with eloquence, you will not learn for yourself. Your spiritual growth will be curtailed. When your body dies, you *will* ascend to one of the Realms of Heaven, but it will be a lower realm because you will have failed to learn for yourself the lessons you were given that life to learn.

You are in control of your own soul's growth. No one else can do it. No one else can experience your various lifetimes, and understand what your soul has learned from each one.

We in the spirit world want you to have knowledge of heaven. We want you to establish your own personal relationship with your God. Seek out the wisdom given from us the spirit world. But seek this knowledge with your eyes open. If you are in doubt of the message or the messenger, meditate on it. Listen to your intuition and your gut feeling. Listen to your own internal sense of right and wrong. Pay attention to your subconscious – that part of your soul that is not entirely of the physical earthly plane but exists slightly beyond it.

Go deep within your mind. Go deep within your heart. Not your physical heart that pumps your blood, but reach deep within the core essence of your being. Not your desires and whims, but go to the part deep inside yourself where you recognize when something is right. This is where God lives inside you. This is where you will find your answers. This is where you fill find truth.

Feel the energy of your God around you. Feel the energy of your God within you. Do not fear death. Do not fear the Universe. Embrace and love your life. Be very honest. Be honest with others. Be honest to yourself and be honest when you commune with your God. There is no truth without honesty. Honesty is the nearest form of being godly.

IN THE WAKE

In the aftermath of COVID-19, now you will be entering a new era. Each one of you will feel you have entered a new phase of your life. It will be very different from what you've known before. You have the opportunity to see this as a pure life, going back to what your life as a human on earth can be. You have the opportunity to reduce the man-created existence guided by the consumer market.

The people who have passed away have learned their lessons, and don't have to be on the earth plane for the new era to begin. Much as it's sad and you are grieving for all the people who have passed away with this COVID -19, they have done their part. They have learned what they needed to learn, and now have passed into the other realms.

Everyone has a different way to cope with losing a loved one, especially if they are young and haven't had a long life on earth. A mother does not expect to lose her child. A father does not expect to lose his child. This is not the usual order, and that makes it even harder to bear. Some of this has been very tragic. But you have had to learn these difficult lessons. One of the hardest lessons you have had to learn is that your life is not a given. It can be lost at any time, at any age. This reminds you of the preciousness of your life on earth.

You've had to re-evaluate. You look at people differently. You look at others wondering if they have the virus. There are many things you are going through.

Towards the end of 2020 people will have a better understanding of the value of life.

The way to cope with losing a loved one is to know that their energy goes on into the other realms. There is no death. Death is just a transition between the realms in between the two life forms where you lose the physical body and take on your spiritual self. Your consciousness does not die. You are very much a part of the Universe in both forms. You will never be away from the Universe. Death is not to be feared, but to be rejoiced.

Going back to the American Indians and other tribes, they would be happy to see their loved ones descend into the spirit realms and into a new life force. It is only society that has told you that God is not a loving God, so you fear death. This fear is man-made. This fear does not reflect the reality of what actually happens when you transition to the other realms. Passing onto the other side is a transition which you will all go through, whether you are a newborn and pass away in your mother's womb, or you live to be 105. It is a transition of the soul that you all will experience many times.

When you meet your maker, the Universe on the other side, will you be accountable for what you have done? Yes, you will. But not to the extent that you will be thrown into some deep, dark hell because that hell does not exist. The fire and brimstone of Hell some people like to evoke does not exist. Would you send your naughty children to such a place? No. Your God would not create such a place. What will happen is that you will be counseled, then sent to come back into the world to learn what you didn't learn the last time.

You will come back in soul clusters, with others that were with you on the previous times. Your mother could have been your lover in a previous life. Or your best friend could have been your father.

The Universe is telling you to sit up in listen. This new era is not the end of civilization. This new era is the end of everything you no longer need as human beings. It is a time to reflect and feel in tune with your spiritual being.

Take away the feeling that you've got to be a size zero or look a certain way. Your body is temporary and will turn into dust. Your soul is what will carry you forward. Your soul is your uniqueness. Your soul is what your creator made. This is what you should nurture.

When you look above you into space, you can see the vastness. You can see there is no beginning and no end. That is the vastness of your soul. There is no beginning and no end. As you pass from the physical, you become whole again. You become one again with the love of the beautiful Universe.

It is sad to lose the life of a loved one. It is a loss of the person's mortal life, but it is a gain of the spirit world. When someone passes away, they have the capacity to sit with you. They have the capability to leave you signs that their soul has survived.

When you take away the physical concerns and look deep inside yourself, all you are is your soul energy. Everything you manifest happens for you. Whatever you ask the Universe for, as long as you are consistent and do it without ego, you will receive. Remember, you are the children of the Universe. You are blessed with life. You are blessed with communication with your creator. You are blessed with a world rich in beauty. You were created from love, and you carry that within you. Do not deny that love. Let it shine within and without. Let it help you heal your world. Embrace it, and be whole.

THE CONSCIOUS AND SUBCONSCIOUS MIND

Your soul has a conscious and a subconscious aspect. Your conscious mind is connected to your physical body. This is located on the physical plane, and involves your everyday thoughts and decisions. This part of your soul is connected to the physical world and your physical body. It is rooted in your brain, and has a purely physical presence. It is heavily linked to your ego.

The other part of your soul is your subconscious mind. This is where you get your subconscious feelings. These are your "gut feelings" and your intuition. You may get a feeling, "I'm not going to do this, it doesn't feel right." This is your subconscious mind speaking to you.

The subconscious part of your soul exists slightly above you, somewhere between the earthly plane and before you get to the first realm of heaven. In other words, it exists in an intermediary position between the physical world and the heavenly realms. It is part of your soul, connected to your conscious mind, so you have access to this throughout your life. However, it is all too often drowned out by your conscious mind and your ego. Your ego wants to dominate and overpower it, just as the egos of others seek to dominate you.

Your first thought usually comes from your subconscious, while your second thought often comes from your conscious mind, heavily influenced by your ego. Remember this phrase: ***Your first thought is Spirit; your second thought is Ego.*** When you "overthink" a choice and change your mind to your second thought, this is often the *wrong* choice.

Pay attention to your intuition. It offers guidance untouched by egotistic constraints. Too many people ignore their subconscious. They ignore their intuition at their peril. They heed their egotistical wants and desires, unaware that this allows them to be controlled by their greed, and by those supplying those things.

You have access to your subconscious mind through its link to your soul. You can strengthen your access to your subconscious mind, through meditation and your prayers and communion with God. Do what you can to nurture your soul, the everlasting part of you. It is easy to be tempted to waste your time and energy on material things that will not last.

But remember that your soul is the part of you that matters. It is very much "real." It is the part of you that goes on long after your body decays and your "treasures" turn to rot.

THE GIFT OF DÉJÀ VU

Déjà vu, a memory flash, means you have an insight of a particular memory. It may be that you dreamed that the situation has already happened. It could be that your subconscious mind in the spirit world has recognized this memory from somewhere else. It is good for you humans to recognize this happens. Déjà vu is a normal process of the human brain and the human soul. When you get that déjà vu moment, it is your subconscious mind reminding you of its power – that you can reconnect with your higher consciousness, which is partly connected to the earthly plane, but also partly outside the confines of the earthly dimensions, including time.

Sometimes you might be in a group, and a few of you could have the same Déjà vu feelings at the same time, that this has already happened. This is a very good thing. It reminds you that your soul, your higher consciousness, exists outside the boundaries of the earthly plane. This is one of the many assurances you have been gifted to remind you that your soul will carry on after your body expires and you pass into the universal realms.

Let me show you a beautiful river, with people enjoying having a picnic. How many souls do you think throughout history have had gatherings and conversations like this? The answer is many. Who is to say that your soul, in a previous life, did not have the same experience and the same type of conversation? As human beings, you like to think you are in control and that you know everything. Unfortunately, you know very little. But your subconscious knows more than you realize.

I want you to picture this – sit yourself down by the river bank. Imagine three friends with you. Imagine the conversation that you are having with these three friends. Then take five deep breaths. With every breath, feel yourself floating higher and higher. Feel yourself floating so high that you are entering a different realm. On this different realm, imagine the same scenario and the same conversation that you had with your three friends. Spend some time doing this simple exercise if you want to recognize and remember and enhance your déjà vu moments.

Here is another exercise about actualizing something that you want through your deeper mind. If you have something important coming up, for example an interview for a job you want very badly, try this. In your conscious mind, play the conversation out on how you want this meeting to go. Then take your five big breaths and connect with your subconscious and play out the scenario again. That way you are giving energy to the Universe on a double level. You can also go up to another realm and start putting the same scenario out. When you attend that interview, certain things will be said that will give you a déjà vu moment.

Déjà vu is a memory stored in your subconscious mind which sometimes filters down into your conscience. Remember, you are all old souls and you come back in soul clusters. Many people who are your friends, your family, your enemies, your haters and your lovers, are the souls of people you have experienced in the journeys of past lifetimes. Someone could have been your mother, your father, your brother, or your wife. But they cannot have been your animals. Your animals have different souls. Their souls are equal to yours, but different. Your dog will only come back as another dog. A snake will only come back as another snake. That's what their soul urge brings them to do.

The soul urge of human beings is to be inquisitive. To be knowledgeable. You have been given the greatest gift to be the caretakers of the earth plane. You have been given the greatest gift of communication – both with each other, but also within your own soul to your creator. Use this gift. Use déjà vu to your advantage. Create a scenario you want to be stored in your subconscious. Allow it to be played in your conscious mind. Direct your thoughts in this way and you will experience it.

ABORTION

I have been asked to address this issue, as it is a complicated one. Abortion, a termination of a pregnancy of a life, is a choice that a soul has to make. I will tell you from no uncertain terms that an ending of a human life inside the body is something that is not taken lightly. Is it murder? Is it relief from a situation? No one has the right to judge. The Universe knows that sometimes things are not acceptable for you human souls and sometimes you have to go through a difficult situation and this is something you must not take lightly.

There are two things you must know. God is a forgiving God, and the soul urge is for life. These two things are not exclusive. When a woman knows she can't handle a pregnancy and would need to abort, the fetus's soul chooses to enter the body of this mother knowing that the mother is not able to sustain the pregnancy. The mother's soul searches hard in making the decision. After termination, the soul of this fetus returns to the spirit world. But you must know that the soul of this fetus has chosen this path to provide a lesson for the mother that she has to learn. If she learns this lesson, the soul of the fetus has done its job.

Nothing bad will come of the mother's decision if the decision was made with integrity. It is painful enough for the mother to decide to end the life for the unborn child.

However, some mothers feel abortion is a type of contraception, and that is not acceptable. Repeating the same patterns and the same mistakes is not acceptable. There is no learning here. The chance for learning is wasted.

Know that the fetus' soul will return and be born again when it chooses to. Also, know that spirit allows you humans to make mistakes. The Universal God allows this to happen. However, the Universe does not appreciate repeated mistakes. When a lesson is provided but is not learned, that demonstrates disrespect. As long as the fetus termination it is not taken lightly, it is not judged upon. But if it is taken lightly, that person's soul will suffer.

This is a strongly-debated subject for you on Earth. Some religions accept abortion, some do not. It is not up to the religion or religious "leaders" to dictate, it is up to the souls of those involved to give it the thoughtfulness such a decision requires. Those involved are the ones who will bear the weight of the consequences. God will not judge if the choice is made with respect and integrity.

If a child decides to come into a mother's body, and later decides on its own that its soul urge is *not* to be born into that soul channel, it is the soul of the fetus that learns the lesson. The lesson can be for the mother or for the fetus – it can go either way.

Sometimes you have to ask yourself if you are making the decision for yourself or if are you being influenced by someone else. Your soul bears the consequences of your actions, and no one has the right to force a decision on you. If a woman is in a relationship with a man who is controlling, and he forced the woman to terminate the fetus, the responsibility is on his soul, not hers. As long as the patterns are not repeated over and over, and are not done through pure anger and selfishness, the Universal God will not judge you for it.

Whatever happens, know that the soul will live on. It will never die. The matter of your body will die. The cells of your body are dying every second. But your soul urge gets bigger and keeps developing. Every time the soul comes back to another body to live again on your rock of earth, it comes back more knowledgeable. We do not look at termination as an easy answer to a problem. But we understand that sometimes it is a means for the mother to go on with her life.

SAME GENDER RELATIONS

The biological purpose of sexual relations, of course, is procreation. But as human beings, you were also given pleasure in the sexual union. Not all creatures on your world experience pleasure during the sexual act, but you were given this.

You have also been given multiple lifetimes, and your subconscious will carry some information from your past lives into your next ones. You may have previously been a man who had a particularly strong and loving relationship with a woman in a past life. When you come back to earth in your next life, you may find yourself attracted to women, regardless of the gender in this new life that you have been born into.

Conversely, perhaps you were a man in a past life who had an unhappy relationship with your wife. This may color your feelings in your next life. In this case, you may find yourself adverse to physical relations with women, despite the gender you find yourself born into.

Your God is a loving God and will not judge you for having physical relations between consenting adults, whatever the gender. God is sad the vessel will not be able to have children, but God understands the reasons for your choices. However, you are not to abuse others. If you perform crimes against others, you will be judged. Crimes against children or animals will be judged harshly.

ARTIFICIAL INTELLIGENCE

Artificial intelligence and robots are things that have been created by man. They do not exist in the spiritual realms. They do not have a subconscious or any connection to the Universal God. They will never have a subconscious mind and will never travel into the Realms of Heaven.

They can never have or take over a human soul. The Universal God will not allow this. What you have to worry about with these robots is what you humans are designing them to do. Be mindful of what you allow them to do and how much interference you allow them to have in your day-to-day lives.

Beware of your electronic devices in your home. Who is watching you through them? Who is monitoring what you do? How much do you want producers of products to know about you? How much do you want government officials to know about what you do in your home? There are many reasons to stem the flow of material desires.

SPEAKING IN TONGUES

When you pray to the Universe, sometimes your soul, in its enthusiasm, wants to speak in the language of the Universe. Some people get the urge to speak in a different format. This can be called speaking in "tongues." This is the language of the Universe.

Do not be alarmed. This is merely a physical expression of the power of the Universe being channeled through you. It is one way to disperse the energy you are channeling so you are not overwhelmed.

WHY YOU WERE CREATED

You were created for a reason. God loves to watch you grow as you love to watch your own children grow. It is a joy for God to watch you learn to take care of each other's souls. You are to enjoy your life. Enjoy your food. Enjoy your experiences. Feed your souls with positivity. This is the glory your God wants for you.

You may wonder why God has not interfered when you harm each other. God has given you free will, and does not wish to take that from you. Would you remove your child's brain so it might not hurt itself?

To help you when you stumble, God sent the ***laws of humanity*** down onto the land. You have been given time to sort your issues out. But over the years, you have become less communicative with each other, as well as with your God. In recent years, some people would rather engage with an electronic text that hear an actual voice.
A serious event has made you stop and take notice of the dangerous direction you were plunging your world towards.

As children of the Universe you have put yourself into segments, and separated these segments into different compartments called religions. You have forgotten that the purpose of religion is to speak to your God, and not to distance yourself from each other. These segments disperse the communities you were born into.

The Universe created you to have the riches provided to you, but you have become very egoistic. You want everything, and you strive to make sure other sectors did not have the same things. This is what the downfall of religion has been -- the fighting amongst yourselves. This was not the purpose of religion.

Go back to the roots of religion – to the laws of treating your fellow human beings with the same respect and care you wish for yourself. Go back to the love of your God. Know that it is your right and your responsibility to speak directly to your God. Do not let some other human get in the way of that. God doesn't want that. Do not let another person tell you they can take you to God if you do what they say. This is wrong. You take yourself to God. God is within you always. Your connection to God is stronger than even your connection to your own life. It is powerful and always there.

There is one word you should have in your universal prayer every day, and that word is gratitude. Do not take your life for granted. Do not throw away your time on earth as if it is dispensable. And do not throw away other lives as if they are dispensable. That is not your place. That does not please your creator who wants to see you develop and grow spiritually.

You all know that children struggle as they learn, but as you struggle to learn, you are equipped with the tools to do so much damage. This only makes it harder for your soul to progress. Do not succumb to harmful actions against your fellow humans. This will harm your own soul's progression.

As with children, sometimes children play with fire or do things than harm themselves, and have to be advised and reminded not to do these things. I remind you, if you do hateful things to others, you cause harm to your soul. You cannot take material things with you when your die. But if you harm others, you *will* take that with you, and you *will* have to deal with the consequences.

The earth is one of the smallest planets, but one of the most destructive. It's as if the human race is God's naughty child. But God has not given up on the earth. Many times, God has wanted to stop you on earth from your destruction, and remove your free will. But the loving energy of the Universal God allows mankind to carry on because God feels that mankind has the ability to learn and get better.

Does this mean that God does not know the future? God indeed knows exactly how bad and how much damage humans are capable of. But because God is a loving God, God wants you to succeed, and does not want to take away your free will.

It's okay to learn. It's okay that you do not have all the answers yet. We in the spirit world have to watch you humans with your fighting, and it makes us sad. But we have to let you live your lives and allow you the chance to grow, or not, as you choose. It's like we in the spirit world are watching a movie of your endeavors. We have to start it at the beginning, and see it to the end. There is much love on the earth but also much destruction, and sometimes it's hard for us to watch.

But the earth is your learning quarters. We have to let you live through this and make the decisions yourselves. Otherwise, you will not have learned.

Does God know how it's going to end? Yes, God does know how it's going to end. This is not for you to know right now, because you must get to this on your own terms. But I will tell you one thing. The human race will not perish. How you will learn not to destroy each other is something you will have to achieve in your own time.

THE UNIVERSE

The Universe is over 137 billion-year-old. Your cosmos, the Milky Way, is a tiny element within this. There are over 50 billion trillion stars. The stars are there to keep everything aligned so that certain planets can obtain life. Not every planet with life will have a sun. There are other energies that create light and warmth for other planets. You have no knowledge of these energies as your minds have been acclimated to understand only the conditions for life on your world. The rest of the Universe is dark matter and dark energy. This is not evil energy; it is simply dark.

In your Bible in Genesis, it says God created the Heavens and the Earth, which is true. Since then people have asked why their souls would we be privileged to walk on the earth plane, to go backwards and forwards through the realms, down and up, depending on the lessons that you are learning and your ability to keep your life pure. Buddhists call this Nirvana. This is the Eternity, with no start, no beginning, and no end.

Your job on earth is to redeem your life. You are allowed to make many mistakes. As you travel up to the other realms, you are accountable for what you have done, and what you are going to achieve next.

The Big Bang had to happen for your world to exist. Right now, there are many Big Bangs going on in the Universe millions and millions of light years away. There are little "bubbles" around life-bearing worlds creating the exactly perfect conditions to sustain life. Your world is in one of these little "bubbles." Your galaxy, the Milky Way, is attached to another much larger cosmos. The umbilical cord of the Universe goes around and around with no time stops and no beginning start. It is there forever.

You are very privileged that God has chosen your individual souls to keep coming down to the learning ground on the physical Earth. When you finally do have your last visit to the earth and have learned and advanced so much, you will dwell above the angels, with God. You will dwell on the right-hand side of God and dwell there forever.

What are the chances that this little rock in the middle of the solar system, which is in the middle of the Universe which goes on above and behind and inside it would have life? Your world did not happen by blind chance, it was created by design. This was designed by the love of your God to provide for you. Not just human bodies, but the animals and plants were created by the Universal Love.

You exist within the third dimension, the conscious dimension. You are aware of your soul. You have choices, and those choices define what you learn and which realm you will go to when your body is done. You control your own destiny. Circumstances come and go, but you control your own fate. This your creator has given you. Your creator has given you life, and awareness, and consciousness. And choices. What you do with your choices is up to you.

What you do now influences what you can do next. This lifetime won't be your last job. You will go back and you will be allocated other jobs, both in the Realms of Heaven, and if/when you return to the earth.

Once you sit on the right-hand side of God, that is when your eyes will be wide open to see and to help other planets that are just developing. If you reach the position of sitting on the left-hand side of God, you will have already achieved this and you will be looking at ways to make life better for these beings on other planets. If you sit at either side of God, you will have reached a level higher than even the angels. Of the billions of souls that have lived on the earth, only a few have achieved this level.

Even we as spirit guides who were once human like you, have not achieved this level. We are more advanced than you, but we have not yet reached that level of purity with complete and total oneness with God. We are still going through a learning process. While we have evolved to the point where we no longer have to return to the learning ground of an earthly life, we spirit guides do not know everything.

Our job is to help you understand what you need to do in order for your souls to learn and progress. We are also on a journey to further the development of our souls. We are further along than you, but we are all on our individual journeys to evolve our souls spiritually.

Are you the first of God's creations? The answer is no. Is your Earth the first planet to sustain life? The answer is no.

Seek the purity in your soul. The more purity you achieve in your soul, the more things you will be able to do. The purer your soul, the further beyond the realms of the angels you will go.

There are millions of planets, but not all sustain life. Your planet happens to be 33 degrees away from everything. If it was a quarter of a degree in a different direction, your planet would not be able to sustain life.

There are over 200 worlds with advanced consciousness. Most of these have advanced spiritually much farther than the human species. For some, this was because their hierarchy was more nurturing in terms of their spiritual growth. Your hierarchy has held you back. The human race is like God's "naughty children." But you are not the only race struggling with your spiritual growth. There are twelve other species in the Universe on their own planets who are also struggling with these issues, and your human race is the seventh of these.

Also, the earth is one of the youngest planets to have evolved a species with advanced consciousness. As children of God, in a way you are like two-year-old children. Think of a toddler. You call this stage: "the terrible twos." This is a good analogy for you to understand where your species is spiritually. In a way, you are just learning to "walk." You have a long way to go before your species reaches spiritual maturity.

God wants you to succeed in "walking." God wants you to learn and grow, and mature and flourish. We spirit guides are here to help you. We are sending you these messages, on how to commune with God and learn to heal yourselves and your world. Other spiritual beings are trying to help you. You have more resources than you realize.

Reach out for these resources. You have untapped power within you. Find it. Release the light inside you. Go deep inside your mind.

GOING FORWARD

We are looking at another doomsday at this moment in time. For you to stay safe on earth, treat others as you want to be treated yourselves. These messages give you guidelines of this new era of your lives – this new chapter of your world.

I've been shown a vision of what God would like your earthly plane to become – full of harmony and full of joy. A world with no lies and no deceit. A world full of beautify energy. God knows that you have had a long time to be consumed and told by the ego of mankind what to do, but now God is giving you a chance to put your earth to rights. You alive on the earth plane now have been chosen to make a difference. You must stand united. You must not get torn by consumer things. You must look at the beauty of what the Universe has given you.

You have been put just the right distance from the sun so that you don't get burned alive. You have been put just the right distance from the sun that you don't freeze. But you are so close to each other because the earth is a very small rock.

If the loving creator can do all this, now you are given another chance to put right what you have been destroying. You must do this. You must try.

Don't worry about the "what ifs" and "what is not." Draw a line in the sand and say, "Now it is time for a new way. The old ways of destruction must stop." Now step over this line, and bring in the brand-new era. Make it how you wish it to be. Make 2020 count as a chance for something marvelous connected with the world.

Don't be obsessed with finding other planets with new life forms. You will not find them. You do not have the technology to do this, and we won't let it happen. It's no good building your million-dollar spaceships to travel to another galaxy. It will not serve you in your human state.

I tell you in no uncertain terms that there is more life on other planets that you can imagine. They are not in the same solar system or galaxy, but they have visited you in the past. They still walk among you today, but your conceptions of them are so wrong. Just remember that you need to know they are there. You don't see them, but they are there. I tell you that you need to trust this, and you need to believe.

Going forward to 2023, if you combined your loyalty to the Universe and channeled your free will for the benefit of your fellow humans, the world will become a better place. You can have peace and harmony, if you want it. If you work for it. You can re-shape your world if you desire it and reach deep inside yourself for it, and work with your fellow human souls to bring it about.

THE SHIFT FROM RELIGION TO SPIRITUALITY

Try to frame your days with a prayer. Develop and embrace your ongoing conversations with God, the spark of God light deep inside you. You could begin each day communing with your God, preparing for the day ahead, and expressing your gratitude for being given that day. You could end each day communing with your God, reflecting on the day and appreciating the gift of it, and the chance to learn from that gift.

There is no special position required for praying. You don't have to kneel or bow or clasp your hands. What is important is that you go deep within your mind and really commune with that part of your soul where your innate sense of right and wrong exists.

For different people there are different ways to know when you have reached that place inside you. Some may feel a sense of inner peace or joy. Some may feel a warm inner glow, or the connection with something greater than themselves. Some may feel the muscles of their face start to relax, as if being drawn into a smile from within. Understand that special feeling when you reach that place deep within your mind where you commune with your God spark.

The more often you go there, the easier you will be able to recognize it. The easier it will be to find your way there again. The more you will speak with your God.

You have been given examples of prayers. These are only examples, given to you so that you understand the nature of the gratitude you should bring to your communion with God. By all means, use these prayers. But don't stop there. Have you own conversations with your God. Don't blindly recite a string of words you have been told to use and expect God will be impressed or appeased.

You are one of God's chosen children. God wants to know your heart. God wants to know what's in your soul. God wants you to embrace the beauty of your life and be grateful, but God does not want robots blindly reciting a pattern of words without feeling.

As God's children, think of God like a loving mother or father. God is like a wise parent who loves the child and delights in watching the child learn and grow.

But like a parent, God does not want the child to come to the conversation with the attitude of, "Dear God, I am reciting these special words I have been told to say. These words will grant me favors and prove that I love you. Words I must say at a special time to prove I deserve favors. I am praying in this special way so that all may see me pray and know I am worthy. So be it, the end. Goodbye for now, until I say these exact words to you again." What loving parents wants this attitude? What loving parents wants rote recitation? The answer is none.

Instead, have a real conversation with God. Ask God your questions. Share with God the richness and fullness of your heart. Ask God how to be a better, kinder person. Feel God's presence deep inside you and marvel, with gratitude, at the loving embrace.

The more you do this, the easier it will be to nurture your soul and allow it to learn and grow. The more you do this, the more positive vibration you give out into your world. The more you do this, the more joyful your present life will be, and the further in the Realms of Heaven you will go next.

NOW is the time to embrace the inner light within you. Religion has prepared your species, like a stepping stone along the way. But religion has allowed you to do terrible things to each other. Take the teachings of religion, if you choose, but transcend them.

NOW is the time to take the next step, to go from religion to spirituality. Embrace your inner God light, and let it shine. After the darkness comes the light. This is your time. This is your chance to shine. We in the spirit world are just starting to see this happen, and we want you to join in.

Know your own mind. Your mind is yours. Enjoy its power, and its freedom. Do not let anyone prevent you from accessing this.

You are the keeper of your soul – no one else can do this for you. You control your soul's destiny. You control your soul's growth. Face your God on your own two feet, with no one else between you. Others may try to get between you and your God but do not let them. Face your God on your own, with courage – the courage of love. Anger is easy, but love is hard.

NOW is the time to go beyond religion. NOW is the time to embrace true spirituality. Your world needs it. You need it. It is yours for the asking. Ask often and freely. Seek and you will find.

This is your charge, and your gift. Go with kindness. Go with God.

Find your inner light, and help light the way.

ABOUT THE AUTHORS

Loraine Rees is a clairvoyant medium in the UK. Her live shows frequently sell out, with little or no publicity, almost entirely by word of mouth. She has helped the British police solve some of their most difficult cases. She does private readings and offers workshops on enhancing psychic connections and abilities.

Dr. Mary Ross has advanced degrees in geology, education, and writing. She met Loraine at a Mind, Body, & Spirit Convention in London. Within 12 seconds of meeting her, Loraine said, "*They* are telling me you're the one to write my books." And so, she has.

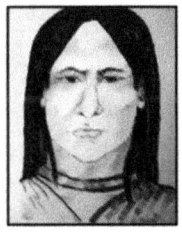

Ramos, Loraine's main spirit guide, was a scribe and counselor for the Egyptian Pharaoh Ramses III, who reigned from 1186 to 1155 BC and is considered to be the last monarch of the 'New Kingdom' to wield substantial authority over Egypt. Ramos was entombed with Ramses III when the Pharaoh died.

www.ingramcontent.com/pod-product-compliance
Lightning Source LLC
Chambersburg PA
CBHW060153050426
42446CB00013B/2809